The Future Foreign Correspondent

Saba Bebawi · Mark Evans

The Future Foreign Correspondent

palgrave
macmillan

Saba Bebawi
Faculty of Arts and Social Sciences
University of Technology Sydney
NSW, Australia

Mark Evans
University of Technology Sydney
NSW, Australia

ISBN 978-3-030-01667-8   ISBN 978-3-030-01668-5   (eBook)
https://doi.org/10.1007/978-3-030-01668-5

Library of Congress Control Number: 2018968255

Cover illustration: © John Rawsterne/patternhead.com

This Palgrave Macmillan imprint is published by the registered company Springer Nature Switzerland AG
The registered company address is: Gewerbestrasse 11, 6330 Cham, Switzerland

For all foreign correspondents who have risked,
and continue to risk, their lives to
tell the truth

ACKNOWLEDGEMENTS

This volume is based on observations stemming from the Foreign Correspondent Study Tour (FCST) which is a project that has been funded by the Australian government through the Council for Australian-Arab Relations (CAAR) to the Middle East and the Australia-India Council (AIC) to India, part of the Department of Foreign Affairs and Trade (DFAT). We are grateful for both CAAR and AIC for their continuous support and consultation. Both the aims of the FCST and its funding bodies were aligned, and this made for a successful collaboration. The authors would also like to acknowledge the Special Broadcasting Service of SBS Online and their continuous efforts in publishing the stories that have come out of the FCST iterations. All the above stakeholders were focused on bridging the connections between Australia and different home countries of its migrant communities. Additionally, without the assistance of local partners on the ground, the FCST project would not have been possible, therefore we would like to thank the Arab Reporters for Investigative Journalism (ARIJ), the Jordan Media Institute (JMI), and the India Institute for Journalism and New Media (IIJNM) for their time and support.

We would also like to thank our colleagues at the University of Technology Sydney (UTS) who have assisted in running, and especially administrating, the FCST, namely: Mariana Baltodano, Destiny Wolf, Brenda Eadie, Karla Price, Krzysztof Komsta and Khatijah Reeks. Thanks also to our faculty colleagues who have enthusiastically supported the expansion of this programme: Peter Fray, Maryanne Dever, Mary

Spongberg and Susan Oguro. The support of the UTS International office has been phenomenal and therefore we would like to thank Simon Watson and Danielle Kowaliw. We would also like to thank Swinburne University in Melbourne for their early involvement, particularly we would like to acknowledge the support of Jason Bainbridge, Stewart Collins, and particularly Andrew Dodd who joined the initial FCST trips and whose valuable journalistic experience helped shape the logistical and professional outputs of the project.

The FCST team has been a fundamental backbone to the project, so a lot of appreciation goes to Krystal Mizzi who is the FCST social media editor, in addition to our local consulting producers: Najat Dajani in Jordan, and Saswati Chakravarty in India. We would also like to thank the FCST film-makers: Juliette Strangio and Dieter Knierim. The study tour leaders are fundamental to the success of each iteration and we thank them for their involvement and their around-the-clock dedication: Devleena Ghosh, Bruce Mutsvairo, Michael Fabinyi and Christine Kearney.

We would like to acknowledge all members of the FCST team for every iteration. It is worth acknowledging that each foreign correspondent intern who attended the FCST made it possible for the idea of this volume to be born. Continuous discussions, observations and learning experiences that each of these interns shared made it clear that such a book was necessary. We would like to thank them for their enthusiasm and willingness to learn. Their reflections and observations made it viable for this experiment to succeed, allowing us to learn more about how future correspondents could be trained, and ultimately how their work could enhance a more global representation of news discourses.

CONTENTS

1 Introduction: The Foreign Correspondent and Journalism
  Today   1

2 Living the Future of News   9

3 Can the Foreign Correspondent Still Exist?   23

4 Reporting Reality   49

5 Transcultural Spheres and the Foreign Correspondent   65

6 The Foreign Correspondent Study Tour   85

7 Conclusion: Future Possibilities   101

References   109

Index   117

LIST OF FIGURES

Fig. 6.1 Syrian refugees (*Credit* Yasmin Noone)   89
Fig. 6.2 Jordanians meditating (*Credit* Yasmin Noone)   94

CHAPTER 1

Introduction:
The Foreign Correspondent
and Journalism Today

Abstract This introduction chapter explains the need for *The Future Foreign Correspondent* book, and how it was inspired through lessons and challenges experienced from the Foreign Correspondent Study Tour (FCST). It briefly explains the concept of the book as a volume that speaks to the future foreign correspondent, examining how they might take an important place in the future of journalism, and crucially, steps that could be taken to train them. It outlines the book highlighting the need to consider more abstract issues and concepts relating to the practice of foreign reporting.

Keywords Foreign correspondent · Fake news · Future of journalism

We are in the midst of a crucial era for journalism. The rise of nationalist and popularist politics in the West has coincided with a deep suspicion of journalistic practice. The basis of that suspicion is not our concern here, though it has thrust the discipline of journalism firmly in the spotlight. Do the long-held tenets of journalism, its status as an objective commentator, still hold? Of course, there has always been biased or partisan journalism, even propaganda, but now some would have us believe the line is blurred across all forms. 'Fake news', a concept that has really existed ever since we started reporting anything to each other at all (Newman et al. 2017; McNair 2017; Stecula 2017), can now be bandied about for political gain, to avoid scandal, or to obfuscate more generally.

© The Author(s) 2019
S. Bebawi and M. Evans, *The Future Foreign Correspondent*,
https://doi.org/10.1007/978-3-030-01668-5_1

Journalists now not only need to find the truth and report it, they need to convince an audience they have done that without prejudice.

As a case in point, in 2018, a dissident Russian journalist, Arkady Babchenko, faked his own death by assassination in Ukraine's capital Kiev. In a complicated ruse involving Ukrainian security officials, make up and pigs blood, Babchenko's death was widely reported on the media with even those closest to him unaware of the contrivance. When he miraculously appeared at a news conference the next day, he had very serious allegations to make about being on a Russian hitlist and needing to undertake these extreme actions to avoid real assassination. This was about life and death for Babchenko. Now this is an incredibly politically charged situation given Russia's annexation of Crimea in 2014, and predictably Russia hit back not only to deny the allegations but to cast scorn on journalistic practice. It was Babchenko himself who called out the ludicrousness of the situation: 'Everyone who says this undermines trust in journalists: what would you do in my place, if they came to you and said there is a hit out on you?' (Reuters, 1 June 2018). In our current mediascape, rather than focusing solely on the extremely serious allegations levelled at them, Russian officials merely deflected to the distrust of journalists' defence. As Matthias Williams (2018) pointed out, it was ultimately the Ukraine that went into damage control, 'seeking to reassure its Western allies'. One wonders if it wasn't a journalist at the centre of the charade whether the dialogue would have been different?

Running parallel to the distrust of journalistic practice has been the greatest technological upheaval since the Industrial Revolution. This has brought into question the necessity of journalists in light of technical alternatives. Already vast slabs of traditional reportage such as sports results, financial reports and the like are being churned out by 'robots' (Lecompte 2015). These algorhythmic reporters are able to synthesise vast amounts of information and present it in summary form for the concerned reader. They do this quicker and more accurately than humans. The reach of these robots constantly extends into more areas of journalistic practice and specialisation. We might question whether these robots are telling stories—more of that later—but combined with the suspicion of journalists outlined above, journalists find themselves in an increasingly precarious situation. It is within this milieu that this volume positions itself.

There are many fine books that retell the stories of brave, inquisitive foreign correspondents and the interventions they made. This is not such a book. The best of those volumes (Dahlby 2014; Greenway 2014;

Borovik 2001; Filkins 2009; Gellhorn 1994; and more) speak to the trials of circumstance, the discovery of information, the dangers of political situations and, of course, attempts to cover up truth. These are important examples of 'life in the field' and sometimes of pre-determined agendas. Obviously many of these accounts are focused around war coverage and use the platform as an opportunity to paint the absurdity of war (see Gellhorn 1994). Others, like Filkins (2009), focus on the collision of religion, culture and modernity, while Greenway (2014) took us to the front lines of politics and war in an unprecedented way. Does the latter still hold the same power it used to? With drones, citizen journalists and even embedded journalists on a 24/7 cycle, we see conflicts (quite visually) in a new way. Still, the canon of great foreign correspondent accounts confirmed what it was to excel in the craft, and what vital exposure they provided. In contrast to the retrospection of these accounts, our volume speaks to the future foreign correspondent, examining how they might take an important place in the future of journalism, and crucially, steps we might take to train them. It considers more abstract issues and concepts relating to the practice of foreign reporting.

To reflect the ideology of the future foreign correspondent, as we will outline later, this book has purposefully connected two perspectives. One of us, Bebawi, comes from experience as a journalist working for CNN and others. She subsequently has become a journalism educator and researcher in university settings. Importantly for this volume she has also established and delivered the Foreign Correspondent Study Tour (FSCT) which is both the inspiration behind the volume and the basis of many case studies throughout the book. The other of us, Evans, has a long history in university management (read thick bureaucracy) and acts more as a commissioning Editor, sending folks into the field for training. He has also turned his attention to examining the disrupted media sector and how various disciplines can reinvent themselves even more successfully within that. We also represent a female/male team and an intercultural one (from Middle Eastern and Anglophone traditions). This is not accidental, it is designed to draw out the tensions and advantages that are naturally present. It also reflects the ideology behind the FCST where an intercultural, inter-difference dialogue is essential to its success.

The FCST is at the heart of this volume. The tour inspired us to develop the lessons learnt and challenges faced into something concrete that could serve other journalists/institutions/educators around the world. In many ways the necessity of the FCST became the necessity for this book. A chance to reflect on new approaches to intercultural reportage, to cultural difference, to creating opinions and understanding. This book covers a range of areas pertaining to the future of the foreign correspondent by revisiting various traditions that have been entrenched in the training and practice of international reporters. We focus on the need for a more diversified intercultural news sphere and the importance of straying away from tried and exhausted portrayals of issues and events occurring in the global South. We talk about the rise, and now abundance, of fake news and how the very existence and role of the foreign correspondent has become crucial in validating facts and reporting reality. We use the FCST experience to note the importance of educating future international reporters on the ground, and how through training there is hope that foreign correspondents might produce fresh and diverse news content. We note the importance of collaborations with local journalists, and even local investigative reporters, who could assist foreign correspondents in getting their facts correct and providing an in-depth account of news, in turn increasing further knowledge about parts of the world that go under-reported. We introduce the notion of 'happy news', to solidify various existing practices and concepts that call for the inclusion of news discourses that *also* offer positive stories of the global South—and not just those of tragedy, conflict and hopelessness—arguing that the role of the future foreign correspondent is to bridge those gaps that still exist between the global North and South. Therefore, this volume is not there is study certain foreign correspondents and their roles, stories and experiences, rather it looks into abstract aspects, issues and concepts relating to the practice of foreign reporting.

We discuss the concept and definitions of 'foreign correspondence' in more detail in Chapter 3, unpacking the pourous nature between the various practices, especially in a more globalised digital media environment. However it is necessary to note that there are various explainations and distinctions between 'foreign correspondence' and 'international reporting', one distinction states that '[c]orrespondents are those who regularly roam', whereas reporters 'tend to work in and around [...] headquarters — either reporting from their desks, or returning to the office after a day in the field to type up their notes' (Lacey 2017). For our purposes, we concur with Kevin Williams (2011) who uses the term 'international journalism' interchangeably with 'foreign correspondence' and will do so in this book due to the porous and borderless nature of media flows today, which we also discuss in Chapter 5.

The book opens by considering the disrupted media sector in which journalists now take their place. It is naïve to speak of foreign correspondents, which immediately conjures up images of the hardened war reporter or the CNN celebrity, without placing that term within the ever-changing, and changed, media landscape. We examine the many technological interventions coming to bear on journalism to see how they can enrich the influence of the foreign correspondent. This scan of the digital influence is vital as we later consider the rise of the citizen journalist, and appraise the possible connection or melding of these journalistic roles.

Following on from this, Chapter 3 asks the vital question: can the foreign correspondent exist in this new digital age? With the world at our desk, do we really need the physical embedded presence on the ground? Clearly we are not the first or only commentators to consider this. And this chapter develops the scholarly arguments that have preceded our ruminations. It goes on to develop the idea that yes, journalists are still needed 'on the ground' but what needs transformation is our entrenched notion of the foreign correspondent. What is vitally important now, also in an unprecedented way, is cultural diversity and cultural awareness. At the heart of the FCST we saw time and again, the growing need for understanding that extends far beyond traditional journalistic paradigms.

Chapter 4 brings us to the realm of reality, a fascinating realm to examine with the current predilection to jettison journalism because of its sham constructs. Indeed, in scenes resembling *The Crucible* journalists are written off daily by political powers for holding hands with the evil that is 'fake news'. It seems everyone has been seen with the Devil, apart, of course, from those being reported on. The role of the audience is paramount here. What is it modern day audiences are seeking from their journalists, and particularly from foreign correspondents? Largely we would argue, it is reality, a true reality understood by the citizens on the ground, not a pre-imagined reality perpetuated for media audiences.

The ensuing chapter presents the fulcrum of our argument: that an understanding of transnational spheres is essential to the future foreign correspondent. Here we focus on the two axis that intersect. The first considers the pre-existing cultures that any journalist consciously or unconsciously brings to bear on their subject. The second analyses, is how that understanding in turn affects the cultural discourse that their journalism produces and the extent to which it can assist in developing transcultural spheres.

Chapter 7 outlines these transcultural spheres as they blossomed through the course of the FCST. Here we provide concrete examples from trainee journalists exploring new ways of living their craft, that involves them moving away from the predetermined way to report a race, religion, conflict etc. A way to break out of the standard discourses that are espoused time and again for various regions or peoples. It also represents a move away from constant negativity towards a connected humanity. How journalists, especially foreign correspondents, represent and communicate a hierarchy of information from what they have gleaned is increasingly vital for how transnational spheres are viewed. The ability to shape the cultural understanding of the news, and the power of that presentation, has never been more potent.

In the conclusive chapter on 'Future Possibilities', we open up the crystal ball on the brave new world of foreign correspondent journalism. We imagine the intermingling of human and machine in redefining cultural norms, and in driving 'happy news' as a means to reinvent traditional understandings of foreign correspondent journalism.

REFERENCES

Borovik, A. (2001). *The Hidden Way: A Russian Journalist's Account of the Soviet War in Afghanistan*. New York: Grove Press.

Dahlby, T. (2014). *Into the Field: A Foreign Correspondent's Notebook*. Texas: University of Texas Press.

Filkins, D. (2009). *The Forever War*. New York: Vintage.

Gellhorn, M. (1994). *The Face of War*. New York: Atlantic Monthly Press.

Greenway, H. D. S. (2014). *Foreign Correspondent: A Memoir*. New York: Simon & Schuster.

Lacey, M. (2017, June 14). What's the Difference Between a Reporter and a Correspondent? *The New York Times*. https://www.nytimes.com/2017/06/14/insider/whats-the-difference-between-a-reporter-and-a-correspondent.html. Accessed 2 June 2018.

Lecompte, C. (2015, September 2). From Nieman Reports: From Earnings Reports to Baseball Recaps, Automation and Algorithms Are Becoming a Bigger Part of the News. *Nieman Lab*. http://www.niemanlab.org/2015/09/from-nieman-reports-from-earnings-reports-to-baseball-recaps-automation-and-algorithms-are-becoming-a-bigger-part-of-the-news/. Accessed 22 May 2018.

McNair, B. (2017). *Fake News: Falsehood, Fabrication and Fantasy in Journalism*. New York: Routledge.

Miller, A. (1953). *The Crucible*. New York: Viking Press.

Newman, N., Fletcher, R., Kalogeropoulos, A., Levy, D. A. L., & Nielsen, R. K. (2017). *Reuters Institute Digital News Report 2017*. Reuters Institute for the Study of Journalism. https://reutersinstitute.politics.ox.ac.uk/sites/default/files/Digital%20News%20Report%202017%20web_0.pdf?utm_source=digitalnewsreport.org&utm_medium=referral. Accessed 16 May 2018.

Reuters. (2018). *Journalist Faked His Own Death Using Pig's Blood and Make-Up Artist*. https://www.smh.com.au/world/europe/journalist-faked-his-own-death-using-pig-s-blood-and-make-up-artist-20180601-p4ziry.html. Accessed 1 June 2018.

Stecula, D. (2017, July 27). The Real Consequences of Fake News. *The Conversation*. https://theconversation.com/the-real-consequences-of-fake-news-81179. Accessed 28 May 2018.

Williams, K. (2011). *International Journalism*. London: Sage.

Williams, M. (2018, June 2). Ukraine's Credibility Under Scrutiny Over Faked Murder. *Sydney Morning Herald*. https://www.smh.com.au/world/europe/ukraine-s-credibility-under-scrutiny-over-faked-murder-20180602-p4zj3j.html. Accessed 26 May 2018.

CHAPTER 2

Living the Future of News

Abstract This chapter provides a broad background to the nature of the current digital media environment journalists are operating in, outlining the scholarly and industry debates pertaining to the challenges and opportunities that this media landscape offers journalism in general, and international reporting more specifically. It lays out the current media landscape by considering the disrupted media sector in which journalists now take their place. This chapter examines the many technological interventions coming to bear on journalism to see how they can enrich the influence of the foreign correspondent.

Keywords Foreign correspondent · Media disruption · Technological interventions · Digital influence

Before we can begin to examine what kind of future exists for the foreign correspondent, it is pertinent to consider the industrial and technological climate in which they will be operating. Much has been made of failings of legacy media in light of digital disruption, and those discussions need not be reprised here (Lim 2017; Neilson and Sambrook 2016). Suffice to say, the sticking point in most cases has been the challenge to existing/traditional business models from online platforms. Crawford et al. note:

> Digital platforms have been drinking the life out of traditional publishers from below the waterline, while the façade of their prey has remained more

© The Author(s) 2019
S. Bebawi and M. Evans, *The Future Foreign Correspondent*,
https://doi.org/10.1007/978-3-030-01668-5_2

or less intact [...] Far from colonizing digital, traditional media's share of the digital spend has in most cases stalled. (Crawford et al. 2015: 2)

Unlike much in the digital world, '[c]ontent creation within news media is not particularly scalable. It's one of the things that makes media companies unattractive in the modern business world. Every news story is bespoke – alive with the detail that makes it unique' (Crawford et al. 2015: 78). Which is further complicated by the digital particularization of the traditional audience: 'The fast-flowing penetration of the internet into all housefuls, and recently into all pockets via a phone, has put an end to the domination of the mass audience' (Kelly 2016: 155). The market for our bespoke offerings is arguably easier to reach, but harder to find. One way publishers are trying to navigate that is by building loyal, committed audiences for their high-quality journalism. The *2017 World Press Trends* report notes that reader revenue continues to grow as the biggest revenue source for publishers, up to 56% in 2016 and 30% of total digital revenue (Campbell 2017: 7). As advertising revenue continues to slide in traditional print mediums (down 8% in 2016 and 26.8% over the last five years [Campbell 2017: 7]), building a loyal readership base is vitally important. As we will show below, the future foreign correspondent building relationships with communities will be a key facet of their role. This chapter also considers other technological and industrial impacts on the future foreign correspondent.

INFORMATION OVERLOAD

This is an unprecedented time to be alive, let alone to try and be a journalist. The sheer amount of information surrounding us is daunting at best. As Kevin Kelly (2016) notes:

There has never been a better time to be a reader, a watcher, a listener, or a participant in human expression. An exhilarating avalanche of new stuff is created every year. Every 12 months we produce 8 million new songs, 2 million new books, 16,000 new films, 30 billion blog posts, 182 billion tweets, 400,000 new products. (Kelly 2016: 165)

The issue is how to wade through all of that information. As Kelly goes on, in attempting to 'triage' the information our 'only choice is to get assistance in making choices' (Kelly 2016: 167). For people curious, interested or desperate for news, that assistance comes in part through journalists. In days past, such assistance was neatly packaged and even more easily digested. We speak here of legacy media presenting news that was heavily curated for distinct audiences. Admittedly the sheer volume of news might have been less than today, but there was still plenty of it, and definitely plenty more than we ever saw or read. Yet, it is often the demise of these forms that is being lamented in this super-connected age. Crawford et al. (2015) point out the vanity of this:

> If plump newspapers and 30-minute TV news bulletins were the only vehicles of truth there might be something [to worry about]. But they are not [...] we have become so used to the familiar formats of news that we think there is something God-given in their forms, something that actually represents the world. (Crawford et al. 2015: 249)

Implicit in this is a warning for us now: Technology will continually change so even the new normal now is temporary. As futurist Steve Sammartino points out: 'Imagine that every single thing that relies on digital technology will be twice as efficient and powerful in 18 months' time' (Sammartino 2017: 45). This alone will have an enormous impact on the amount of information available. No doubt the speed of access to this information will alter how people consume it. Social media platforms, or information jugganauts, continue to rewrite the way we exist as humans: 'What it is within Facebook's power to know is unprecedented in human history. Facebook is sitting on the biggest trove of data about the things we value most in the world – ourselves and our relationships' (Crawford et al. 2015: 114). Hence there is a logical panic around technology, particularly new social media technology, and its effects on society, politics, radicalization, isolation, youth health and wellbeing, and more.

Part of the conjecture around the relationship between technology and journalism obviously concerns the former's possible decimation of the latter. A *2016 World Economic Forum* report on the future of jobs forecast that 'around 65 per cent of children starting primary school today will end up working in jobs that don't yet exist' (Sammartino 2017: 47). So will journalism be one that does still exist, and further to our context here, will the foreign correspondent? We will address this more in Chapter 3, but for now it is important to remember that: 'All jobs are eventually displaced or changed by technology. Technology-driven unemployment has always been a fixture of the human experience' (Sammartino 2017: 47). Understanding the change, and how journalists can work proactively with the change is vital. Implicit in this is the future training and education of journalists. We focus on this in Chapter 6, but there is a need to be clear about the change that is taking place. Steve Coll, Dean of the Columbia Graduate School of Journalism, summarises it best:

> It was very tempting, in many ways necessary, for journalism schools to rush over to the teaching of tools, the teaching of platforms, the teaching of changing audience structure. But that transformation often had little to do with the core, enduring purpose of journalism, which is to discover, illuminate, hold power to account, explain, illustrate [...] What we're really seeing now is that this is a durable change in the structure of information, and therefore a need to durably change a journalist's knowledge in order to carry out their core democratic function. (quoted in Berret and Phillips 2016: 29)

As the structure of information has changed, along with its distribution and our access to it, so must journalists adapt their craft and knowledge base. Jeff Jarvis argues that the 'key question journalists must ask today is how they add value to the flow of information in a community, a flow that can now occur without mediators – that is, without media' (Jarvis 2014: 5). This is an important understanding of the change. Jarvis is not interested in journalists as the source, the only source, of information, or even in bite sized packages of news. As 'news' floats down the massive river of data that now exists, how do journalists add value as it passes by? For some, exploration of new forms or foci of journalism have been forefront of mind. Jim Macnamara writes that:

> Alternative models of journalism such as public and civic journalism, as well as evolving forms such as interactive, participatory, networked, and citizen journalism, are designed to broaden the range of voices that receive a megaphone through media and broaden the range of viewpoints and interests represented in media. (Macnamara 2014: 27)

Thus one value add these new, changed forms of journalism might bring is greater diversity, but also an amplification of the voices often not heard (see Chapter 5). Whether the broadening of viewpoints has really occurred yet is debatable, particularly in Western media.

One area where journalists have clearly been able to add value is through culminative data, specifically as applied to data journalism. Data journalism is broadly 'the application of data science to journalism, where data science is defined as the study of the extraction of knowledge from data' (Berret and Phillips 2016: 15). The purpose of which is to join dots and tell stories, or as Macnamara puts it: 'being able to combine, compare and analyze large amounts of data to gain insights and identify patterns and trends' (Macnamara 2014: 46). Columbia University Graduate School of Journalism considers data journalism to be pivotal to the future journalism profession. In a pioneering survey of data journalism instruction in tertiary US settings they note:

> To place data journalism in the core of journalism education will mark a crucial advance in what schools can offer their students. Journalists who understand data and computation can more effectively do their job in a world ever more reliant on complicated streams of information. (Berret and Phillips 2016: 8)

Here again we see the 'streams of information' and the question of how journalists can add value to that. Placing such skills at the core of journalism education is bold, visionary but also the kind of essential adaptation journalism will need to take to survive and prosper into the future. In thinking about foreign correspondents one could argue that the flows of data are even deeper given the vast political, cultural and religious elements that might be involved. Yet it is naïve to view these developments in big data sets as being exclusively important to journalism. Berret and Phillips point out that across other (more) traditional disciplines, adding value to the information flow is more and more important: 'Like data journalism, computational work in the humanities and social sciences is growing, and this is reflected in the relatively healthy academic job market for digital humanists compared with the job market for traditional scholars' (Berret and Phillips 2016: 27).

Related to the power of big data to tell new, revelatory stories is the power of the crowd to create value. The modern journalist has unprecedented access to a social collective and adds impetus to storytelling through their utilisation. Thus it is important they realise this crucial function in their day to day practice. It is no longer just about their view, about their own story template: 'So our job isn't only to inform the public. It is also our job to help them inform each other' (Jarvis

2014: 21). Kelly agrees, '[i]t is not necessary that we invent some kind of autonomous global consciousness. It is only necessary that we connect everyone to everyone else – and to everything else – all the time and create new things together' (2016: 274). Kelly explicitly addresses Jarvis' question about adding value here—it is by creating new things, and for foreign correspondents, new knowledge and awareness. The daunting part is connecting people, allowing them to inform each other. And perhaps this is the new direction for foreign correspondents, acting more as conduits than authorities. 'The sum outperforms the parts' (Kelly 2016: 140), and here is a key message for future foreign correspondents to remember: Not only is it necessary to seek out all the information flows but it will be your job to join many of them together. Collaboration is crucial, and relationships are vital—this is not a job for robots. Jarvis would see the relationship aspect as paramount to all future journalism: 'As we in media build new skills around relationships, we must first stop seeing people as a mass. We need to know them, then serve them as individuals and communities' (Jarvis 2014: 16). He would go so far as to say this is the metric by which successful journalists should be measured. And why not? If you cannot find and connect communities, bring out their stories and connect them to relevant others, then in the current age you have not achieved your goal. For foreign correspondents this should be the lifeblood of their journalism, and new technological platforms provide the means to create these connections. Relationships, however, take time, they take connection. They are not something that can be entirely developed and maintained from afar. Thus, the future foreign correspondent needs to be in the middle of these relationships, and physically present where possible, and attuned to local nuances continually.

For Jarvis, and with justification, the measure of success for journalists should be relationships. Not the number of followers, likes, friends or connections, but real relationships. Journalists need to begin to view themselves 'as enablers, sometimes educators, even organizers and, yes advocates. We change how we measure our success – on the number, depth, quality, and value of the relationships we build – and how well-informed and well-equipped people are as a result' (Jarvis 2014: 24–25). Some argue this focus on relationships is being replicated by major news publishers as well: 'The business model is shifting from selling eyeballs to advertisers to selling journalism to readers […] key metrics have moved from pure scale in favour of loyalty, retention and building community' (Campbell 2017: 18).

WHO WRITES THE NEWS?

The dominant technological feature of our age has been the rise of user generated content. This has fed and catapulted online platforms like Facebook, YouTube, Instagram and others into the global behemoths that they are today. But citizen involvement has also radically changed the way news is experienced. As Williams notes, 'the most significant change is often seen as the rise of individual websites and blogs and other forms of user-generated content (UGC). The mobile phone, email and text messages have communicated a considerable amount of international material to news organisations and agencies' (Williams 2011: 81). Williams here, drawing the direct connection to international news, is highlighting the new information sphere that foreign correspondents must transverse and synthesise in their everyday experience. User generated context is now vital to the construction and dissemination of news.

A Pew Research Center Project for Excellence in Journalism study in the US found that '37 percent of Internet users have contributed to the creation of news, commented on news or disseminated news via postings on social media sites such as Facebook or Twitter' (cited in Macnamara 2014: 48). And this sharing culture has had a profound effect. For one, it has transformed importance via popularity, as Crawford et al. note: 'sharing on social networks has become a major distribution mechanism for news stories' (Crawford et al. 2015: 5). Yet, as they go on: 'Like all distribution mechanisms, social networks influence the content they distribute. It turns out that people on social networks prefer certain styles and types of content' (Crawford et al. 2015: 5). Thus, social media has created the scenario where certain news styles are preferenced and others abandoned all together. The increasingly personal algorithmic solutions that deliver our news in these formats means that unbiased global reportage is harder to find for some people. The future foreign correspondent is pitted against these localised, personalised forces in attempting to disseminate their messages. The sharing culture, however, is making this harder, not easier. Crawford et al. (2015), having embarked on a three-year project entitled 'Share Wars' that digitally tracked the most sharable news stories on the internet and classified them via a bespoke taxonomy found that, despite their original optimism, the sharing culture had not produced a more authentic, powerful, collectively emboldened news delivery. As they more poetically put it: 'Three years on, the world has changed. Our original hypothesis – that sharing would make news better -- looks as naïve as the 1970s promise of sexual freedom' (Crawford et al. 2015: 281).

On a more positive note though, it is in some ways now easier to break the traditional reportage cycles, especially those pertaining to 'bad news'. As Williams notes, 'new content producers such as bloggers can eschew the negative news values that pervade the coverage of international news and provide different forms of representation. The online world no longer requires that national perspectives dominate' (Williams 2011: 83). This is a huge benefit to the future foreign correspondent and one that needs to be harnessed, as we argue in Chapter 5 through the notion of 'happy news'. The traditional, sensationalist, stereotypical view of countries and peoples need not be the norm. Online vehicles allow for balanced reporting but also localised voices to have greater prominence. While we know that traditional media have agendas that disproportionately disadvantage international news, with online user generated content this can be more counter-balanced. As Williams puts it: 'Commercial broadcasters do not reflect the social commitments that characterize public service media, and with foreign news perceived as low down in the interests of audiences they have cut back on their provision of international news' (Williams 2011: 85). Online 'broadcasters' have no such restraints or hierarchies, and are free to publish as detailed and localised analyses as they desire. They may choose to entirely reflect certain social commitments at the expense of more traditional newsworthiness.

TECHNOLOGY AND THE TRUTH

One clear repercussion of the rise of UGC has been the growing uncertainty around truth. Crawford et al. suggest that this has become particularly prevalent since 2014, around which time:

> a whole industry had grown up around the creation of fake articles designed specifically to be shared on Facebook. Many of the offending mastheads are name to impart authority: *National Report*, *Civic Tribune* and *World News Daily Report*. Most have a professional look and feel [...] The headlines are believable and play to the biases of certain readerships. (Crawford et al. 2015: 217)

They go on to note how, particularly in an Australian context, producers of such material are making far more money than they used to as objective journalists. Furthermore, readers have become increasingly drawn to such news sources, as Campbell notes:

In 2016 [...] it became clear that news outlets deliberately publishing untrue stories were seriously influencing public opinion. In the autumn, with the US election drawing near, Facebook figures showed that fake news sources were now outperforming mainstream media in terms of user engagements for the top 20 election stories. In other words; people were turning to stories that confirmed their own political bias – disregarding any journalistic merit. (Campbell 2017: 13)

So the confluence of money, exposure and increasing influence has fertilised these sites and seen them proliferate. Williams noted in 2011 that it was 'estimated that nearly 56 per cent of active blogs are splogs: faked blogs designed to trick advertisers and search engines' (Williams 2011: 139). That figure would not have improved much today. Future foreign correspondents will need to navigate this territory astutely. Kelly sums it up most powerfully:

For every accepted piece of knowledge I come across, there is, within easy reach, a challenge to the fact. Every fact has its antifact [...] Ironically, in an age of instant global connection, my certainty about anything has decreased. Rather than receiving truth from an authority, I am reduced to assembling my own certainty from the liquid stream of facts flowing through the web. Truth, with a capital T, becomes truths. (Kelly 2016: 279)

If there are multiple truths out there on any issue, particularly when intercultural sensitivities are involved, then how does any foreign correspondent navigate that? Moreover, how do they present a version of events that is heard and accepted by the majority? Kelly himself answers this earlier in his volume: 'When copies are free, you need to sell things that cannot be copied. Well, what can't be copied? Trust, for instance. Trust cannot be reproduced in bulk?' (Kelly 2016: 67). Trust is produced by relationship. By continual, consistent, proven relationship. To return to Jarvis, this should be the metric by which human journalists are measured. Future foreign correspondents will need to work in both virtual and physical spaces to build that trust, thus enabling their stories, and their connections between people are viewed as authentic and reliable.

Looking deeper into the crystal ball, one finds unexpected territory for future foreign correspondents. It revolves around the world of virtual reality (VR). What if (and really it is a when) foreign correspondents are able to be in another place remotely, without physically occupying it. In speaking of a similar space, Kelly writes, 'one of the weirder apps I found is one that will float the dollar value – in big red numbers – over everything you look at. Almost any subject I care about has an overlay app that displays it as an apparition' (Kelly 2016: 232). So if any subject can be overlayed, then news, sources, geographies, conflicts, houses, camps, parliaments etc. obviously can be. In this situation the journalist's influence is external, but with some grounded authority that has built up over time. It is germane, therefore, for the journalist to be present, to be providing the overlays, so that there is context to any agenda-driven scenario presented. Here the foreign correspondent becomes fundamental to a world that is overlaid with someone else's information. This is the world we have already entered, and future foreign correspondents will need to be prepared and present in such a world. A world where the foreign correspondent is as present virtually as physically is what they need to be trained for.

One of the holy grails it was hoped technology would deliver is in the area of fact checking. Macnamara notes that most fact-checking initiatives (e.g. FactCheck, PolitiFact, Fullfact) were based around political environments, specifically the checking of speeches and political statements, but did not 'research media content more generally' (Macnamara 2014: 43). Kelly outlines the prosumer ideal that could be part of every household: 'Besides automatically correcting the spelling and critical grammar, Google might also fact-check the statements in the letter with its new truth-checker called Knowledge-Based Trust' (Kelly 2016: 127). Here individuals might benefit from a fact-checking function, but what of larger media corporations or journalists more generally? Founder of *PolitiFact Australia*, Peter Fray, feels that the most powerful interventions in fact-checking are going to come from artificial intelligence:

> In both the process of fact-checking as an emergent journalistic 'truth-telling' practice and the much more traditional process of uncovering and forming facts there is no doubt that artificial intelligence offers journalists exciting ways to increase the available pool of facts and apply greater analytical and contextual rigor to those facts. (Personal communication with the author, 30 January 2017)

Furthermore, this engagement with artificial intelligence could alter the way facts are perceived and even archived:

> By harnessing the power of AI and machine learning, journalism and collaborative disciplines have the potential to add a new dimension to how

facts come into the public space, how they are received and consumed in that space — and what happens to them thereafter. (Personal communication with the author, 30 January 2017)

Moreover, the notion of fact-checking extends further than simply verifying the claims made by public figures. One of the great challenges facing journalists (and the general public), in the future, is ascertaining the veracity of sources/people/groups online. Even Kelly concedes that it is 'very difficult to determine how real someone online is' (Kelly 2016: 235). Here again we see the need for foreign correspondents who are embedded, physically and culturally ensconced. They have more potential to recognise falsity and be aware of those creating it. But this is an increasingly cloudy area, and increasingly the work of experts. As Kelly notes:

> If a person online did not have any friends on social networks, they probably weren't who they claimed to be. But now hackers/criminals/rebels can create puppet accounts, with imaginary friends and imaginary friends of friends, working for bogus companies with bogus Wikipedia entries. (Kelly 2016: 235)

Once again there is the possibility of pitting technology against technology in this instance through the enhanced use of artificial intelligence: 'Smart machines could make the addition of new layers of transparency and accountability to journalistic output quicker, easier and cheaper than is currently and humanly possible' (Peter Fray, Personal communication with the author, 30 January 2017). It becomes more about partnership between technology and the future journalist, rather than substituting one for the other.

Thus, we see it is crucial for the journalist to be on the ground, to be embedded in real communities. Only real relationship within real communities (whether they be physical or virtual) will potentially weed out this subterfuge. While this may even become beyond the reach of the foreign correspondent, they represent one hope for the presentation of fact over fiction. Jarvis contends that one way this could happen is to provide platforms to the public that enable truth-telling. He suggests that 'perhaps our first task in expanding journalism's service should be to offer platforms that help individuals and communities to seek, reveal, gather, share, organize, analyze, understand, and use their own information' (Jarvis 2014: 21). This would certainly go some way to weeding out the falsity that exists online. The suggestion of a platform here goes beyond normal business operatives. And to that end it is a tricky suggestion. But the notion of a collective platform that produces informed localised information is both informed and increasingly important. However, Kelly contends that a purely egalitarian platform is not necessarily the answer. He is convinced there needs to be some oversight, some editorship: 'To get to the best of what we want, we need some top-down intelligence too. Now that social technology and sharing apps are all the rage, its' worth repeating: 'The bottom alone is not enough for what we really want. We need a bit of top-down as well' (Kelly 2016: 148). So what is the role for any journalist, let alone a foreign correspondent, in this? Surely they represent the 'top-down' in this scenario? Anderson et al. (2012) would argue this exactly: 'The journalist has not been replaced but displaced, moved higher up the editorial chain from the production of initial observations to a role that emphasizes verification and interpretation, bringing sense to the streams of text, audio, photos and video produced by the public' (Anderson et al. 2012: 22). This is a significant broadening of the understanding of the journalist's position amidst the onslaught of information. It also represents a significant challenge for the future foreign correspondent. The training for this top-down role is increasingly fraught—and is something we will return to later in this volume.

HUMANISE THE TECHNOLOGY

There is no doubt technology will radically alter the profession of journalism, and the role of the foreign correspondent. But it would be a mistake to view this as mere substitution. There remains an important role for every journalist, and especially for future correspondents—they will be the ones who humanise the technology. As Sammartino notes, 'the best UX [User Experience] designers I've met haven't been the best techs, but rather the most empathic' (Sammartino 2017: 49), and so by extrapolation it could be with journalists. They will not need to understand every line of code in the technology, but they will need to be able to speak to people who do. They will need to understand the multitude of parties who are engaging with the technology, and bring empathy to their stories. This is not to say it will be easy and seamless, nor is it on the agenda tomorrow. As Peter Fray notes:

The development of practical and non-threatening partnerships between human and machine in the journalistic space has a long way to go. Some existing jobs will be lost, some diminished and many reconfigured. But new jobs will be created, possibly more than will be lost. Better still, smart machines offer new ways for journalists to listen to and talk with audiences. (Personal communication with the author, 30 January 2017)

The future foreign correspondent is a very human role, one that can ultimately be enhanced by technology rather than destroyed by it. It is important to work with the technology and not be paralysed by it. Sammartino again notes, 'it is vital we do not let the fear of new technology overcome the economic and social power it offers us. This revolution is kinder, more human than the last one' (Sammartino 2017: 72).

REFERENCES

Anderson, C. W., Bell, E., & Shirky, C. (2012). *Post-industrial Journalism: Adapting to the Present*. New York: Tow Centre for Digital Journalism, Columbia University.

Berret, C., & Phillips, C. (2016). *Teaching Data and Computational Journalism*. New York: Columbia Journalism School.

Campbell, C. (2017). *World Press Trends 2017*. Frankfurt: WAN-IFRA.

Crawford, H., Hunter, A., & Filipovic, D. (2015). *All Your Friends Like This: How Social Networks Took Over News*. Sydney: HarperCollins.

Jarvis, J. (2014). *Geeks Bearing Gifts: Imagining New Futures for News*. New York: CUNY Journalism Press.

Kelly, K. (2016). *The Inevitable: Understanding the 12 Technological Forces That Will Shape Our Future*. New York: Penguin Books.

Lim, S. (2017, September 27). Legacy Media Organisations Are Paying the Price for Slow Pivot to Digital Disruption, Experts Say. *The Drum*. http://www.thedrum.com/news/2017/09/27/legacy-media-organisations-are-paying-the-price-slow-pivot-digital-disruption. Accessed 30 June 2018.

Macnamara, J. (2014). *Journalism & PR: Unpacking Spin, Stereotypes and Media Myths*. New York: Peter Lang.

Nielson, R. K., & Sambrook, R. (2016). *What Is Happening to Television News?* Digital News Project 2016. Reuters Institute for the Study of Journalism. http://reutersinstitute.politics.ox.ac.uk/sites/default/files/2017-06/What%20is%20Happening%20to%20Television%20News.pdf. Accessed 15 May 2018.

Sammartino, S. (2017). *The Lessons School Forgot*. Milton, QLD: Wiley.

Williams, K. (2011). *International Journalism*. London: Sage.

CHAPTER 3

Can the Foreign Correspondent Still Exist?

Abstract This chapter questions whether the concept and role of the foreign correspondent still exists in light of the digital media environment that reporters operate in today, with the rise of social media where users have access to events on the ground. This chapter includes a discussion on various scholarly debates on this, arguing that there is still a need for reporters on the ground to report on events, albeit that the concept of the foreign correspondent might need to change within an ever-changing media environment. At the same time, there is a greater need for cultural diversity as positions on global media discourse state, hence the need for more cultural understanding.

Keywords Foreign correspondent · Global journalism · International reporting · Parachute journalism · Local reporter · Citizen journalism

It was during the first trip for the Foreign Correspondent Study Tour (FCST) in 2015, when the question of whether there is currently a need for foreign correspondents or not was raised. At the offices of the *Gulf Times* in Dubai, the FCST media interns were meeting with the newspaper Editor In Chief, and as they were explaining their role as foreign correspondents during the study tour, another editor standing at the door was quick to sarcastically ask whether the concept of the foreign correspondent was still relevant, making us all question what we were doing!

© The Author(s) 2019
S. Bebawi and M. Evans, *The Future Foreign Correspondent*,
https://doi.org/10.1007/978-3-030-01668-5_3

To many reporters and journalists working around the world from their desks with access to immediate online sources, information and social media, the concept of the foreign correspondent seems redundant. Journalists can reach any source they want through online calling tools such as Skype, Facetime or Zoom. Crowdsourcing has replaced vox pops on the streets through social media such as Twitter. And any information—almost any—can be accessed online. Williams (2011) comments on this noting that '[t]he growth of the internet, with its provision of instant access to databases and information around the world, reinforces the "stay at home tendency" of modern foreign reporting [...] foreign editors are more reliant on their online sources of information' (Williams 2011: 139). Furthermore, trusted bloggers and citizen journalists can provide unique footage from any location and even report on events on the ground, as seen through the 'Arab Spring' protests where major media outlets were partnering up with prominent citizen journalists on location.

So the whole 'why be there at all' argument is a valid one, and the question of whether a foreign correspondent is still required in today's media environment continues to persist, especially in light of the financial restrictions facing many media organisations which are tightening their budgets, and where foreign correspondents are the first to go when financial cuts are made. Yet online journalism is hard to verify—a point which will be discussed in detail in the following chapter on 'Reporting Reality' and as discussed in the previous chapter. Nonetheless, despite the slow down in the recruitment of foreign reporters by Western media organisations, foreign correspondence is expanding in parts of the global South. Richard Sambrook (2010) notes that the decrease in the number of foreign correspondents is a Western phenomenon that is not necessarily being matched in other parts of the world such as Asia, for example, which is undergoing economic growth. Sambrook argues that this noted growth will lead to an independent form of journalism in the developing world, which will in turn affect global news flows and the nature of public debate in relation to these parts of the world (Sambrook 2010: 1). This ultimately impacts the role of foreign correspondents who have traditionally had to travel to developing countries that did not have their own outwards facing media, and which formed parts of the silent media from the global South (McChesney 2003; Murdock and Golding 2005; Rai and Cottle 2007).

Accordingly, with the decline of foreign reporting in some parts of the world, and its possible expansion in others, the question remains centred on the extent to which foreign correspondents exist in light of the current media environment. This is especially so with the rise of social media where users have access to events on the ground, and in light of economic restrictions on news organisations that were once a beacon for foreign correspondents. This chapter will include a discussion on various scholarly debates in relation to this, arguing that there still is a need for reporters on the ground to report on events, albeit that the concept of the foreign correspondent might need to be transformed and reconceptualised within an ever-changing media environment. At the same time, there is a greater need for cultural diversity that needs to be reflected in foreign reporting and which has always been somewhat lacking, as Chapter 5 will address. This current chapter, therefore, will first unpack the role of the foreign correspondent as traditionally practiced and discuss some limitations to the role. We will then outline some current issues that are entrenched in international reporting as a result, followed by a discussion on what the future of the foreign correspondent might need to entail based on these issues, thus setting the basis for this volume. It is necessary, however, to highlight that it is not within the scope of this book to give an account of the historic developments of foreign reporting, since other scholars have written comprehensively on this (Hamilton 2009; Williams 2011; Sambrook 2010).

CONCEPT AND ROLE

Although news now circulates in an online environment where it is instant and travels beyond borders, at this stage there is still a clear distinction in the literature between national, foreign and global journalism, and it is therefore necessary to clarify these distinctions. Peter Berglez (2008) explains these differences, stating that *domestic* news is focused on 'intranational' and relates to local, regional or national news; *foreign* news on the other hand is focused on reporting on events from either another country or a transnational region; whereas *global* is news that connects issues or problems that concern different countries or regions around the world (Berglez 2008: 854). Although these distinctions are tied to different journalistic content, we argue that foreign or international reporting needs be redefined, taught, and practised to reflect and focus on establishing the commonalities and interconnectedness of discourses between the national, the foreign and the global.

There are many scholars who have questioned these distinctions as a result of a changing media environment. For example, John M.

Hamilton and David D. Perlmutter (2007) have argued that 'demography, ideology, and technology challenge the assertion that news can be categorized as "foreign" versus "local"' (Hamilton and Perlmutter 2007: 9). Williams (2011) also emphasises the porous nature between foreign and local news, where he sees that there are many discussions which ignore the 'porous borders' between the domestic and the foreign. Williams is critical of the term 'foreign reporting', since '[t]he word 'foreign' implies that what is reported is alien, strange and unfamiliar' (Williams 2011: 21), which is due to historical ties with news being a product of media systems that are situated and constructed within nation states, and which 'have been have been organised on a national basis serving the informational needs of the state, commerce and civil society' (Williams 2011: 21). He explains the historical context to this:

> Foreign news comes in different shapes and forms and the gathering, reporting and dissemination of international news has been undertaken by a variety of actors in a range of organisational contexts serving numerous objectives and interests [...] The centrality of national interests, needs and considerations to the emergence of the media ensured that international news would be defined as news about and between nations. (Williams 2011: 20)

Ulf Hannerz (2012) provides additional context to the concept of foreign news in relation to the 'national':

> The simplest reading of "foreign" in "foreign news" is certainly that it refers to news from abroad, reported across national boundaries. In that sense, one may view it as a spatial notion; but it is a matter of space already socially constructed and regulated. Again, we can also entertain the idea that it involves news that is somehow alien, strange — that such news has crossed boundaries of understanding and is not unproblematically accessible in cultural terms [...] But not everything in the news from elsewhere is so easily grasped. Words, words, and more words may be required for an understanding. (Hannerz 2012: 32)

The idea that news from other lands is alien and not easily grasped by target audiences as outlined by Hannerz, and the focus on national interests when reporting on foreign news as discussed by Williams above, stresses that there is a disconnect between cultural representations and realities from the countries being reported on and the audiences being reported to—a point we discuss throughout this volume. A more cultural bridging of news discourses could address this disconnect or notion of 'alieness' that has come to symbolise foreign reporting throughout the years. In turn, a more cosmopolitan attitude is required at both ends of the production and reception process of international news making.

Hannerz (2012) discusses the concept of cosmopolitanism at length in relation to foreign reporting. He notes that what foreign correspondents tend to do is report on a country through a frozen time and place, what has become known as breaking news. This snapshot in time is not considered the normal state of affairs in that particular place. In turn, what this reporting fails to communicate is that life goes on as normal just as any other place around the world after the event, thus failing to create a sense of cosmopolitanism (Hannerz 2012: 33)—a sense of commonality. Accordingly, Hannerz argues towards replacing the term 'globalisation' with 'cosmopolitanism' when thinking of foreign correspondents, as the concept of globalisation is more economically defined whereas cosmopolitanism has been associated with 'transnational interconnectedness'—a point we also make throughout this book. Hannerz explains here what he means by 'cosmopolitanism' as:

> a more cultural and experiential conception, referring to an awareness and appreciation of diversity in modes of thought, ways of life, and human products and to the development of skills in handling such diversity. This cosmopolitanism, we should note, does not intrinsically refer to national units; it may relate to diversity in the world or in one's neighbourhood. (Hannerz 2012: 21)

This diversity needs to be reflected in the reporting of foreign correspondents, where the interconnectedness of discourses should become a priority in international reporting. Interconnectedness has been discussed in the literature, for example Simon Cottle (2009) sees that journalism, in general, is becoming 'interconnected, interdependent and communicated in the complex formations and flows of news journalism' (Cottle 2009: 309). Here Cottle talks about the dissemination and movement of news flows—yet to what extent is this increasingly globalised nature of news reflected in the interconnectedness of *discourses* in the current practice of foreign reporting?

The impact of the digital sphere on foreign correspondence is not the only factor that needs to be reconsidered in current and future practices of foreign reporting, historically there have been fundamental issues to the practice of foreign correspondence that need to be revisited, and in turn challenged, such as discursive gaps in the reporting of transcultural spheres as we discuss in Chapter 5. These issues, which have traditionally been entrenched in the practice of foreign reporting, have consequently obstructed the lines that define what the role of the foreign correspondent should entail. Foreign correspondents have, over the years, taken many approaches to reporting from location, and which in turn have affected the quality and veracity of their reporting. To illustrate, John Herbert (2013) talks of a French correspondent who describes foreign reporters through three categories: the first is the foreign correspondent who can be seen to take on a 'tourist' approach, staying for a few days, barely scraping the surface. The second type of journalist is the one who takes on a reporter role by spending more time in the location, however is still not engaged with the issues or the people, and who 'allowed the idea of themselves as "war correspondents" to get in the way of telling the story'. The third type of journalist is further engaged, spending more time and putting in effort to get the real story by digging deeper, and who as a result is in higher risk of dying. Despite this, it is essential to note that risk and potential death should not be the sole markers of deep engagement with a local culture. The study tour experiences that we discuss in Chapter 6 were only limited to two weeks, however, the journalists were strongly encouraged to dig deeper and make connections with the people and the country.

The work of foreign correspondents, in turn, should not be about their experience but about relaying the story of local issues and people. We see on international networks, the big (often white) TV personality jetting into the devastated region (especially within natural disasters or conflicts), and bringing their charisma, their reputation, effectively their story to the story. It becomes about them being there! James Rogers (2012) states in his book on *Reporting Conflict*, that in some cases 'a journalist tries to become the story, rather than report it' (Rogers 2012: 118). The foreign correspondent's experience, therefore, needs to differ from that of a visitor or tourist outlining their experience with the place. They need to find and understand local issues, research them and unpack them, talk to locals and uncover their interpretations of events and issues. Ideally, foreign correspondents need to be embedded in that culture and the political context for a period of time, or if not possible, at least actively acquire in-depth knowledge over the short period of time spent on location. They must aspire to fully know and understand the environment they are reporting on all levels. The aim is for their reporting to lead to a change of perceptions for an audience who does not have access to the same experience and information flows. In essence the foreign correspondent is mediating the events on the ground—that is their role.

The role of foreign correspondents is also shaped by their training. Herbert (2013) raises the point that foreign correspondents have often worked as domestic reporters who are not trained to report on foreign locations and, in turn, lack the cultural understanding and skills required to do that. This again makes their role as mediators limited since, as Herbert states, foreign or global journalists 'are expected to use their transferable skills learnt doing domestic stories' (Herbert 2013: 61). The lessons learnt from training participants during the FCST iterations, are strong examples of how future foreign correspondents need to be trained to focus on intercultural reporting that is different from the training they receive when reporting in their home countries. As Herbert points out above, foreign correspondents tend to not have been trained in international reporting, and instead transfer their journalistic skills as domestic reporters which, in turn, limit their ability to provide a cultural understanding when working as foreign correspondents. The learning experiences from the FCST discussed in this book somewhat illustrate that although the participants were learning on the ground, the cultural nuances would have still been lacking without the instruction and training provided to them whilst they were there. Although it is not within the scope of this volume to analyse existing work by foreign correspondents, we have relied on personal experiences, observations, and existing literature to establish the need for the above issues to be integrated further into the work of future foreign correspondents.

The implications of not training future foreign correspondents to report in international settings are clearly problematic as such training does not maximise the media power (Couldry and Curran 2003) foreign reporters potentially hold to mediate what is actually happening on the ground. Such power, due to their proximity to events on the ground, allows them to refute dominant discourses and in turn construct counter-discourses. Hugo de Burgh (2005) questions why reporters are not taught how to use the power that allows them to mediate reality:

> If journalists have power in the constructing of public discourses, how are they taught to use this power? [...] When news reporting can lead to decisions on whether or not to go to war, we are all affected by the power of journalists and how they mediate our world. (de Burgh 2005: i)

The power that foreign correspondents have, therefore, in the construction of 'social reality' (Couldry 2000; Boyd-Barrett 2002)—discussed in detail in the following chapter—means that it is crucial that they develop the ability and skills required to navigate and communicate transcultural spheres. This power is fundamental to the role of the foreign correspondent. When we consider the power that international news organisations have in global conflict reporting, such as CNN through what has been labelled as the CNN-effect (Robinson 2011), then the role and power of the foreign correspondent is magnified.

Hence, the power that foreign correspondents hold is conditioned by their proximity to events and their ability to witness what others cannot. Many scholars have articulated the role of the foreign correspondent as 'bearing witness', as Sambrook (2010) explains:

> For decades, foreign correspondents had fulfilled the dual role of reporting news of interest to their audiences at home and analysing and commenting on those events in a way which gave their organisation a distinct point of view. They had enjoyed the position of being the principal source of information from far-flung lands. More than that, through eyewitness reporting, they served a public purpose in bearing witness to major events. (Sambrook 2010: 10)

Still, without the immersion in local issues, positions, and beliefs, the concept of 'bearing witness' is limited since foreign correspondents traditionally only report on what they perceive and what they see. How often have we watched reports showing foreign correspondents standing and reporting from the location or event, describing what he or she sees, and drawing conclusions based on that? Reports carry an 'account' of what foreign correspondents experience, linking it to hypothetical reasoning and assumptions. One study based on the discursive analysis of different reports by CNNI, BBC World, and Al Jazeera English on the same event, revealed that each news organisation, and even each reporter from the same organisation, reported on the event based on their personal perceptions and views (Bebawi 2016). The perception of the foreign correspondent based on personal experience is narrow and limited, and the viewer is led to believe that this is a holistic understanding of the event or place. A notable example of this was the reporting of the first Gulf War (1990–1991), where journalists were confined to the rooftops of Al Rasheed hotel in Baghdad, and in turn all images of the war were coming out of that one angle of the city. The viewers could see the occasional bombing with dust during the day and green flashes during the night. Although it was live and real, and was an example where audiences experienced war in real time for the first time (Johnson 2015), it was not an accurate and holistic account of the war or the place. In turn, defining the role of the foreign correspondent through the notion of 'bearing witness' is potentially limited, unless they provide a holistic account of the situation and not a mere description of one perspective or camera angle.

It is important, however, not to assume that the foreign correspondent has complete autonomy over his or her work. In addition to editorial constraints, foreign correspondents are also subject to institutional, government or different forms of authoritative control, and this should be kept in mind despite the arguments made in this book. Williams (2011) notes this: 'The relationship between foreign correspondents and the government has become more complicated [...] which has made the foreign correspondent more vulnerable to physical threat and psychological manipulation' (Williams 2011: 130). Arguably, therefore, it is imperative to rethink what is meant by foreign correspondence, what that role entails and what the limitations are, especially within an increasingly globalised media environment. More importantly, and what this volume explores, is the need to revisit some practices and approaches to foreign correspondence that are required to ensure accurate reporting of actual reality rather than a constructed limited reality. The next section will expand on some of the current issues in international reporting.

Issues in International Reporting

There are some practices that have traditionally been entrenched in foreign correspondence and consequently continue to affect international reporting despite the advent of new technologies. While John Maxwell Hamilton and Eric Jenner (2004) argue that foreign correspondence has changed in the way it is reported and consumed as a result of economic constraints and technological innovations, we see that there are practices that remain in place that impose challenges to the discursive content of how information is conveyed. This section will discuss some of these traditional and recent practices to international reporting, looking into the pros and cons and the issues associated with them through the FCST experiences.

Pre-conceived Story Ideas

Foreign correspondents often go to the countries they are meant to be reporting on with pre-conceived story ideas, particularly when these story angles are dictated to them by their editors back home. In fact, international reporters are encouraged to start working on their stories, lining up interviews, and pitching stories prior to arriving to their destinations. Although this could work for documentary-based reporting since research is necessary for such an in-depth form of journalism, it can be problematic when reporting with the aim of *uncovering* events or stories on the ground. If foreign correspondents go to a country with pre-conceived ideas then this leads to reproducing the same types of stories, and consequently does little to challenge dominant discourses or expand the global public sphere. It can also mean that foreign correspondents become blind-sighted to any stories that arise whilst on the ground as they are too busy pursuing their pre-conceived stories.

This is what was observed during the FCST experiences, whereby the training journalists failed to see fresh news stories—and they were plentiful—as they were focussed on chasing the stories they had pitched prior to arriving on location. This is not to say that research is not required before reaching a country, and certainly there is a need to be hitting the ground running once foreign correspondents arrive to a new destination, however there needs to be flexibility and openness to learning and understanding what the place has to offer otherwise foreign correspondents would not need to travel and instead could just report from their desks.

The agreement that the FCST project had with SBS allowed training journalists to pitch stories before departure and also during the study tour. However, students felt the need to have all their stories pitched before they go, this of course meant that they were finding story ideas and angles based on Google searches and scouting existing news articles and events on the destination. While this remains a valid and useful method of finding stories, it certainly limits the opportunity to uncover unknown and new stories. FCST participants voiced this concern during the study tour where they said that they wished they had left some stories to pitch whilst at the destination, as there they found that they were coming across different, unusual and unknown stories every step of the way. Pitching stories beforehand is common in the industry and that is why there is, more than often, a replication of stories in different variations which can be labelled as 'fads', such as stories on women's rights in the Middle East, or poverty in Africa. These 'fad discourses' not only lose their impact on audiences over time, but also lead to the creation of a limited mediated public sphere, where only particular discourses circulate with different variations, locations, and characters.

One of the issues that training journalists faced during the study tours was that commissioned stories from the editors in Australia came with detailed feedback and instructions on how the story would be executed and produced beforehand. Such feedback included particular instructions on what sort of images were required, detailing locations, sights, colours, and even characters. This of course was problematic as it meant that FCST participants were trying to execute the story requirements imposed by editors. Training foreign correspondents were asked to include certain angles and images from the perception and imagination of the editors based on their own experiences of what foreign reporting looks like. The FCST participants, in turn, were concerned that they could not match these images. An example of this is when one FCST participant was asked to film an interview of women running businesses from home in Jordan, and the editor had asked the participant to include detailed requirements such as the need to film one business woman talking from her living room that reflected a particular cultural setting. Upon arrival to Jordan, the participant said that the interviewee had changed the location of the interview to a business training centre for women as the interviewee preferred not to be filmed at home for cultural reasons. This meant that the requirements requested by the editor were not met and the student was therefore concerned. In response to this, the instructions given by the study tour leaders to the reporters were to follow the story as is. The role of the foreign correspondent is to report on stories as they are and as they come, reflecting the reality on the ground, as will be discussed in Chapter 4, and not based on pre-orchestrated productions of stories.

Foreign correspondents need to go into a country or a place with open eyes, looking for topics, stories and angles that aim to enhance the discursive news space. One exercise that has proven to be useful during the FCST experience illustrates this. Participants are told to keep one day free and are briefed in the morning on a location or village they will be reporting on. This briefing, however, is intentionally short and vague, as the participants are told to find stories on the ground for a period of three hours, upon which they are required to return and produce various stories by midnight that day that make up a multimedia package (see https://social.shorthand.com/fcstudytour/u2cjNJBISHu/al-karama). This has proven to be an authentic experience for participants by emulating to some extent the 'breaking news' scenario. The challenge in this exercise is finding stories on the ground and with very little research in addition to dealing with the issue of language barriers, yet as a result interesting stories emerged. One participant comments on this:

> Despite the challenging nature of this task, it taught me that I had the strength and ability to overcome an unfamiliar and confronting task. It also reinforced the fact that I need to be more observant/responsive to my environment, as there are stories everywhere. (Participant E)

To demonstrate the kind of stories that emerged, one participant walked into a village in Bangalore during the February 2018 FCST iteration and noticed that all the villagers were washing their clothes in tubs outside their doors, women carrying buckets of water, cows being washed, and even some people brushing their teeth outside their houses. After some questioning, the participant found out that the water comes to the village once a week, uncovering an interesting story about the shortage of water supply to the village and the consequences of that (https://social.shorthand.com/maary_mra/3CfWG3mUx3/gollahalli). This is an example of a story that would not have been possible for the participant to pitch from her desk in Australia. The need for foreign correspondents to report without pre-conceived story ideas, and even story angles, is essential for both expanding the discursive mediated sphere and mediating new discourses within transcultural spheres.

Although this seems an obvious requirement for a foreign correspondent—or a journalist for that matter—many reporters fail to see their role as working on stories based on what the location offers. Rather they report on preconceived angles, or pre-set editorial dispositions, and try to fit their sources within those parameters. Herbert confirms this:

A vital part of news selection and decision making for all journalists, particularly those working in foreign countries away from their base newsroom, is a firm focus on what the assignment is; an idea of the story reporters are looking for. Sometimes, newspapers decide the angle, headline and tone before the facts are gathered. The global reporter's job often is to make the facts fit the headline. (Herbert 2013: 35)

This, of course, becomes problematic as it results in a lack of understanding of the actual reality on the ground, and in turn leads to stories being reported that repeat the dominant discourse in relation to that location. Thus, the stories that challenge the dominant discourse are never told, and intercultural discourse is never established.

Parachute Journalism

When a significant event occurs in a particular location, there is an influx of international reporters to the scene wanting to cover the event in real time, all competing to get the story first. This is where the term 'parachute' journalism has stemmed from, as it reflects how reporters 'drop in' to the location they are meant to report on, adopting more of a fly-in/fly-out approach. This journalistic practice clearly has its limitations as not only do parachute reporters often have little or no understanding of the location they are reporting on, which is in turn reflected in their journalism, but it could also potentially endanger them if they are not aware of the local environment and politics. Such was the case with the Australian reporter Peter Greste who after a few days in Cairo freelancing with Al Jazeera, found himself arrested on 29th December 2013 as part of a bigger political information war between the Egyptian government and the Qatari news channel (Bebawi 2016: 152). Greste ended up being incarcerated until 1st February 2015. Generally, there have been distinctions and tensions between different types of journalists reporting on international news such as 'fulltime and freelance reporters', or 'the long stay reporter and the parachute journalist' (Williams 2011: 23). Williams argues that:

> With correspondents' spending less time in their regions familiarising themselves with the background, history and culture, they are increasingly unable to question or challenge the ideological values or stereotypes that underpin the processes by which news is produced. (Williams 2011: 107)

Yet there are reasons why parachute journalism has been common, since it is not feasible for news organisations to have reporters planted in every country. Even though bureaus of major news organisations exist in politically active parts of the world—such as the Middle East or Africa— reporters find themselves having to cover vast regional areas and multiple countries that differ politically, socially and culturally. Having said this, reporters who have stayed in one place for many years and thoroughly understand the culture and the political context of a place, have also been critiqued for becoming too involved in local politics by taking sides and producing unbalanced reporting. This was the case of Robert Fisk who was the 'resident' Middle East correspondent for *The Independent* during the 1980s in Beirut, and who was accused of adopting biased journalism and being pro-Arab in his reporting (Cooke 2008). This can become an issue, as being too entrenched in a particular country or region as a foreign correspondent could potentially obscure their reporting, however it still provides a far more in-depth form of reporting than what parachute journalism has to offer.

Although two weeks for the FCST might not be enough time, at least it allowed journalism students to know that other journalism cultures and news perspectives exist, which in its own right is a significant and essential requirement for foreign correspondence. One participant notes:

A challenge I learnt was that time restraints and pressures of journalism are evidently significant, however this increases drastically for a foreign correspondent. Having to write in a foreign country can be a challenge especially with deadlines in place. Being able to spend two weeks in India, I was able to learn a lot about Indian culture, however I learnt this isn't a luxury which all journalists have. Furthermore, language barriers were one of the major challenges which I faced throughout this trip. From making calls, interviewing and transcribing, not knowing the local language was a struggle which I learnt, makes the job of foreign correspondents very difficult. In order to overcome this challenge, developing relationships with locals is essential for all journalists. This was the only way I was able to understand and transcribe my interviews. Communication is one of the most important skills for a journalist to have, because their job is to communicate with all types of people and communities. This experience has taught me that building relationships is essential and in order to do this, you need to be passionate and dedicated to everything you do, despite not always connecting to every person or story. (Participant L)

What we are arguing here is the need for foreign correspondents to be aware and actively seek to report on different discourses, representing other cultural news angles, and bridging gaps within transcultural spheres as discursive connections need to be made through news reporting despite the time constraints that foreign correspondents face.

One element which has been raised by Geoff Mungham (1987) and noted in Williams (2011), in relation to traditional practices of parachute journalism is that such a form of foreign correspondence is seen 'harder to control or hold accountable' (quoted in Williams 2011: 136). Williams notes that '[t]hese reporters feel fewer obligations to accede to ground rules and arrangements and are less concened about incurring the disapproval of the local authorities' (Williams 2011: 136). This in essence is a good thing, since different to long-term resident foreign correspondents, local governments and authorities do not always have the power to control or monitor the work of parachute journalists, especially if they publish their stories after departing the country or location. This, of course, has somewhat changed in a digital media environment, however it still remains a viable point in many parts of the world as we discuss in the following chapter through the example of the Philippines investigative journalists who were working with the Reuters foreign correspondents covering the drug war.

Source Validation

One common issue with reporting in general, and foreign correspondence in particular, is that journalists tend to take what their sources say at face value, not necessarily questioning the validity of what they say. This tends to happen when there is limited knowledge of the political, social, economic and cultural contexts surrounding events, and reporters more than often do not realise that their sources might be providing misleading or incorrect information. Foreign correspondents also tend to rely on tried and tested sources, especially using the same sources without questioning their knowledge, as noted previously. The reasons behind this is that it is easier to use sources that are known to converse well in English, for example, and who speak well for the media, especially if they are an authority figure. However, relying on the same sources means that news discourses continue to be limited and, more than often, inaccurate. Jamie Matthews (2013) talks about this:

The diversity of perspectives represented in the news is central to questions of balance, accuracy and impartiality. By relying on a small number of sources, journalists risk relaying misleading information as news while, at the same time, permitting these sources to shape the boundaries of interpretation around an issue or event. (Matthews 2013: 244)

The main issue with this is twofold: sources—including people on the street—will tell reporters any views or positions that protect them, especially in political settings during times of conflict or turmoil, where they do not want to say anything against authorities or groups in power that could put them in danger; and the second issue is that sources would want to provide their version of the story that either benefits them or sits in accordance with the narrative they prefer to convey.

An example of this is illustrated during one FCST experience when two Australian students were conducting a story on women's liberation movements in Jordan during the November 2016 iteration. They had interviewed one female feminist academic who was known to be outspoken for women's rights in Jordan. They provided a draft of the story where she was claiming to be the first to initiate a women's liberation movement, and accordingly they framed the article stating that women in the Arab world were finally declaring their rights. This, of course, was not true as it dismisses all the previous work Arab feminists had historically done, including the sacrifices that they had made. The problem in this scenario is not only that the Australian reporters had not done their research, but they also took everything this academic had said as true. They believed the academic to be accurate, especially since news discourses on the Arab world tend to paint a bleak picture of women being submissive and powerless. Although this could be true to some extent, women's liberation movements in the region has a long history of successes that was completely neglected in the article. Accordingly, the FCST participants were asked to spend more time researching historic feminist movements in the Arab world, fact checking what the academic had said, and finding new sources to interview. The result was an article that had a closer representation to reality, with an opening line of '*Feminism is not a new thing in the Middle East*' (see https://www. sbs.com.au/topics/life/culture/article/2016/11/15/what-being-feminist-means-arab-world), a point that also relates to discussions from Chapter 4 on how foreign correspondents need to report reality.

One of the FCST reporters who worked on this article reflected on the experience by saying:

> We talk about journalists needing to be objective but I think we need to talk about an interviewee's objectivity, or lack thereof, too. I will return home with the understanding that interviewees bring their own agenda to a story and it is up to the journalist to fact check every word they say and scope out the big picture of the story beyond what an interviewee might tell me. (Participant H)

This is also an example that supports the need for foreign correspondents to be culturally aware of the locations they report on in order to accurately relay reality, and the need for them to question and validate what sources say is an essential part of that, as we will discuss in the following chapters.

The Local Reporter

One of the practices that foreign correspondents adopt in order to gain a better understanding of the place they are reporting from is to work with local reporters. This, if done well, could yield positive results. Here we refer to local reporters as either freelancing or employed journalists in the country being reported on, and not 'fixers' whose roles are seen more as 'local producers' (Murrell 2015: 2). Recently local reporters are becoming more equipped and skilled, and are consequently taking on the roles of foreign correspondents, as news organisations are becoming increasingly aware of the value of local reporters. As an example of this, Al Jazeera has employed both a mix of Arab and Western foreign correspondents. Speaking to Sambrook (2010), the Reuters' Editor of Political and General News at the time, Sean Maguire, noted the conscious shift to employ local reporters:

> We employ a lot fewer Brits than we used to as we shift further away from the old colonial/commonwealth model of white males spending a career moving from assignment to assignment. Staff is much more likely to be female, younger and nationals of the country they work in. Apart from cost, issues of equity and fairness in employment are driving that shift. Additionally news consumers [...] demand higher levels of instant expertise in reporting – to deliver that you need correspondents who speak a

local language, are immersed in local political and economic life and have contacts developed over years. (quoted in Sambrook 2010: 48)

This was then supported by his Editor-in-Chief, David Schlesinger, who stated that Reuters has a team of reporters from 90 different countries, believing that local journalists have the knowledge and expertise in reporting local stories in association with the key players and local context—in other words: 'They know their areas' (Sambrook 2010: 48–49).

One limitation to local and foreign reporters working together, however, is that local reporters lack the protection, safety and immunity that foreign reporters generally have. Sambrook notes that '[l]ocal staff may be subject to social or political pressures that outsiders are not; simply by virtue of living in a local community they may be less inclined to report critically about their home country' (Sambrook 2010: 52). Bunce sees that due to structural changes in the news industry, discussed in Chapter 1, there has been a shift towards the demise of the foreign correspondent altogether and an increased reliance on local reporters (Bunce 2015: 497).

It is problematic however to rely solely on local reporters, despite their wealth of knowledge, as they do also bring their own local prejudices which means local stories are not necessarily reported on through an un-biased frame. This was noted in the FCST experience, where local Indian reporters who partnered up with Australian journalists to work on local stories found it hard to distance themselves from their own prejudices, despite them consciously trying to do so. To illustrate this, a collaboration between one FCST media intern and a local MA journalism student at the Indian Institute for Journalism and New Media (IIJNM) was conducted in Bangalore in February 2018, where both media interns worked on a story on African migrants in India. The story was not only interesting because it explored migrant waves from one country in the global South to another, but also because it focused on racist tendencies and frictions between the African migrants and the local Indian society. In this situation there was an Australian training foreign correspondent working with a local training journalist. They both set out to visit and interview African migrants in their Bangalore suburbs over a period of one week. The Indian journalist had never set foot in these parts of Bangalore and was therefore apprehensive. The Australian journalist, on the other hand, had no issue with this as it was all new and 'foreign' to her. Due to the sensitivity of the topic for the Indian journalist, and in turn the discomfort associated in researching the story, during the interviews the Indian training journalist kept asking to leave and cut the interviews short as she felt that the responses from the African migrants on racism by the Indian society were a direct attack on her. The Australian journalist, on the other hand, denied these requests by the Indian journalist as her curiosity led her to persist with the questioning during the interviews, finding the responses both intriguing and useful for the story. Following are the comments made by the Australian FCST training journalist on her experience working with an Indian local journalist who we refer to as 'X' in this instance:

Her presence as an Indian – and mine as a white Australian – created an interesting dynamic when we interviewed an African student named Paschal. [X] clearly felt uneasy as we walked through the run-down neighbourhood where Paschal lived. As Paschal directed us up the narrow stairs to his small unit, [X] seemed scared, reluctant to spend time with him in a confined space. Yet I was unfazed, more intrigued by the unfamiliar surroundings than unsettled. Throughout Paschal's angry account of his experiences of racism and hardship in India, I repeatedly ignored [X's] assertions that we had enough information, a little annoyed she was rushing me to finish the interview. [X] was visibly relieved when we left Paschal's flat. Yet later that day, when we talked to another African student who had much more positive experiences in India, [X] seemed a lot more comfortable and happy to spend time with him. Even when we listened back to our interviews in my hotel room, [X] told me just looking at the video footage of Paschal made her feel scared. It was only later I realised [X] felt Paschal was talking directly to her when he was accusing Indians of being racist and attacking him, and when he vengefully stated he'd make Indians living back in his home country feel just as unwelcome. Whereas I, a white Australian, didn't feel this same sense of being personally attacked. This experience gave me greater insight into the tensions between the African and Indian communities: Indians may feel accused and villainised, while Africans may feel angry and ignored. It also showed me that foreign correspondents have a valuable role to play in journalism: I'm not sure Paschal would've been as candid if I – an outsider – hadn't been there. And it highlighted the need to handle the topic sensitively in my article, finding a delicate balance between capturing the opinions of the African community while also portraying Indian perspectives, without creating a simplistic narrative of Indian racists and African victims. (Participant C)

This comment by the Australian training foreign correspondent above provides an insight into how the dynamics of working with a local journalist unfolded. Having said this, the above experience was also a

learning experience for the local Indian journalist, who later in an editorial meeting noted that she had gone back to her friends and community
to say that they had been conditioned to believe that African migrants
were dangerous and aggressive, when in fact they were also suffering
from prejudices. She also stated that she would never have selected this
story to report on had the Australian journalist not suggested it, and was
therefore now a topic she would be keen to cover in further detail for the
Indian media (Participant J). This is an example that reflects the importance of foreign correspondents working with local reporters on local
stories, and which was a beneficial experience for both. Particularly, had
the local reporter not sat in on the interviews with the foreign reporter
and addressed the topic from a different angle with different questions,
the local reporter would not have diverged from the standard angle. It
was an opportunity for the local reporter to also learn more about part of
her city she did not know about.

One of the FCST participants to India, however, came from an Indian
heritage and she found it hard to find stories as it was all too common
for her. In contrast to her other counterparts joining the FCST to India,
she did not see the local place, issues and culture through a fresh eye
so she was less intrigued. This places some emphasis on the importance,
again, of collaborative work between local reporters and foreign correspondents, where the outside reporter brings in new and fresh perspectives that often become too naturalised for the local reporter. The local
reporter, on the other hand, provides context and accurate representations to the foreign correspondent. This was particularly noted during
the FSCT iterations when it came to translating interviews and contextualising viewpoints and perspectives. FCST participants noticed difference
in the story framing when their interviews were translated in relation to
context, especially when there was the need for terms and expressions to
reflect the original meaning intended by the interviewee to a global audience as opposed to word-by-word translations. The cultural gap, therefore, is minimised when interviewee's expressions and way of thinking
it translated by local knowledge in a way that makes sense to a global
audience, resonating within a common human expression. This bridging of the cultural gap is achieved through a successful collaboration,
therefore.

Various cultures of journalism, as we will discuss in Chapter 5, also
come to play in such collaborations between foreign and local reporters.
One FCST participant noted that working with local Indian journalists

exposed them to other journalism cultures, which they described as 'passionate and proactive' – elements that they were not used to in their journalism training. This participant states:

> Working with local journalists at the International Institute of Journalism and New Media (IIJNM) added another enriching layer to the FCST. It was helpful to see their working style, how they 'do' journalism and how passionate and proactive they are. (Participant D)

This also reflects that collaborations between foreign correspondents and local reporters allows them to be exposed to different journalism cultures and ways of doing journalism. It emphasises that there is no universal method of doing journalism, and that journalists could learn and benefit from each other's journalistic skills and approaches. More importantly, working with local reporters allows foreign correspondents to learn a way of doing journalism that is contextual within the place they are reporting from.

Therefore, getting local reporters to work with non-local reporters ensures—at least theoretically—that any prejudices are avoided in news discourses produced. The Associated Press (AP) has been practicing this; it has moved 'from a traditional mode of ex-pat correspondents to a more equal partnership with local staff' for more effective outputs, believing that a mix of local staff and foreign reporters is more effective, as in essence '[i]t provides coverage that is authoritative but also open to the curiosity that a non-local may have' (Sambrook 2010: 49). This leads to both parties questioning each other in pursuit of stronger coverage, providing insights and varying perspectives. This might also lead to foreign correspondents learning to change their attitudes and expanding their perceptions. The notion of foreign correspondents working with local reporters is not new, however foreign correspondents have not always listened to local knowledge and instead stuck to their news agenda. Hence foreign reporters must have the capacity and attitude to adopt local views if this cooperation were to succeed.

Citizen Journalists

It is necessary to acknowledge citizen journalism as one of the main challenges to foreign correspondence today. It is not within the scope of this book to discuss this phenomenon at length as there are many scholars who do outline the implications of citizen journalism on foreign reporting (Hamilton and Jenner 2004; Sambrook 2010). Yet it is one challenge that is worth mentioning here in relation to the question this chapter poses, which is: does the foreign correspondent exist today? Prior to the rise of citizen journalism, foreign correspondence was only taken on by major news organisations, this was because: '(a) people seek out familiar sources that they can trust for news; (b) only large, traditional news organizations have the structure and funding to cover foreign news exhaustively and accurately; and (c) true "foreign correspondents" are by definition employed only by conventional media organizations' (Hamilton and Perlmutter 2007: 10). Yet, as a result of the rise of the citizen journalist, or 'amateur foreign correspondent' (Hamilton and Jenner 2004: 311), international reporting has often had to rely on these sources especially during times where access to events and conflicts has not been possible for foreign correspondents.

During the Libyan civil uprising, which led to the ousting of president Muammar Gaddafi, and which started on the 17th February 2011, the Libyan government was quick to close off all conflict zones to foreign reporters who, as a result, were blocked from reaching these areas. Foreign correspondents, in turn, reached out to citizen journalists on the ground via social media to access information and footage. This was an interesting change of power, where foreign correspondents no longer had control over the veracity of content they were receiving. This was evident in televised reports that would consistently include disclaimers before viewing footage stating that sources could not be verified (Bossio and Bebawi 2012). This was a very different approach to what had previously been seen from the foreign correspondent reporting on the ground, providing crucial evidence and convincing arguments. Despite having citizen journalists report on events that would have traditionally gone unreported, the veracity of the content remains an issue. Williams (2011) sees that online technologies have weakened the power foreign correspondents once held in being the sole source in international reporting. He states that:

> The proliferation of news and information outlets brought about by technological change has had the most profound impact; it is seen as marginalising the traditional foreign correspondent, making him or her simply another source among a variety of sources of international news. (Williams 2011: 94)

On the other hand, Hamilton and Jenner (2004) argue that in fact the digital media environment has enabled the work of the foreign correspondent, providing more possibilities for both the sourcing and dissemination of news:

> We present evidence here that the correspondent, endangered though s/he may be in the traditional setting, is flourishing in new environments. The operative metaphor is evolution, not extinction. As the new media environment inhibits the traditional foreign correspondent, it makes it easier for the dissemination of other types of foreign correspondence. (Hamilton and Jenner 2004: 303)

Despite both these views on whether digital platforms could lead to the extinction or extension of the work of the foreign correspondent, digital technologies have certainly created a very different environment to that where international reporters once operated in. It could be the case that how the new media environment affects the survivability of foreign correspondents is dependent on how they utilise it.

Overall, the issues discussed in this chapter outline just some of the challenges that threaten the foreign correspondent today. There are, however, other challenges that have been noted by scholars. Sambrook (2010) outlines some of the others challenges to foreign correspondence and news organisations in his work, and these include:

- Adopting new roles as the value in foreign reporting shifts to the extremes of breaking news and in-depth specialism.
- Rethinking the international agenda as news values change and 'bottom–up' priorities emerge; using digital technology to broaden coverage.
- Entering new partnerships with a more open and networked approach as vertically integrated news operations break down.
- Innovating in the digital sphere or risk being outflanked by new entrants.
- Finding new economic models which can sustain international operations.
- Training and recruiting to provide the expertise and cultural flexibility needed in the twenty-first-century news arena. (Sambrook 2010: 2)

Sambrook discusses these challenges in detail, however as technology changes and the media environment develops new challenges will continue to emerge. In light of all the above challenges, the question remains whether the foreign correspondent still needs to exist?

THE FUTURE MODEL?

It is very difficult, if not impossible, to predict how the media environment will continue to develop, and in turn what challenges will be facing international reporters in the future. Many scholars have attempted to understand what the future foreign correspondent will look like, and whether this profession would become redundant or not? Hamilton and Jenner (2004) have mapped a model for future foreign correspondents which they have placed in the following categories of the foreign correspondent: Traditional foreign correspondent; Parachute journalist: Foreign correspondent; Local foreign correspondent; Foreign local correspondent: In-house foreign correspondent; Premium service foreign correspondent; and Amateur correspondent (Hamilton and Jenner 2004: 313–314). Although this model provides a comprehensive mapping of the different 'ways' international reporting has evolved, it still does not reflect how the discursive content should be shaped or how it can ensure the reporting of reality—an issue we discuss further in the following chapter.

Sambrook states that '[i]n future, foreign correspondents are likely to be far more diverse in gender, ethnicity and background. They will speak the language and have specialist knowledge of the country before they are eligible to be appointed' (Sambrook 2010: 100). Sambrook argues that a 'white middle-class male' foreign correspondent might no longer be sufficient to bridge cultural gaps, due to the increasing interconnectedness of information around the world. He states:

> The growing interconnectedness of the world, through global communications, ease of travel, increasing migration and more, is changing expectations of international reporting. What was once 'foreign' is now better known. For diaspora communities, news from overseas can be news from home. In increasingly multicultural societies, national identity is more complex and a white middle-class male reporter may not be an adequate cultural bridge between the country he is reporting and the audience at home. (Sambrook 2010: 47)

In this book we argue that one important role for the future foreign correspondent is bridging the cultural gap between the global and the local, in turn emphasising commonalities across cultures. This volume will look into some areas of which the foreign correspondent would need to adapt to a more globalised and intercultural world. It questions past practices and aims to better understand the challenges facing future international reporters.

References

Bebawi, S. (2016). *Media Power and Global Television News: The Role of Al Jazeera English*. London: I.B. Tauris.

Berglez, P. (2008). What is Global Journalim? *Journalism Studies, 9*(6), 845–858.

Bossio, D., & Bebawi, S. (2012). Reaping and Sowing the News from an Arab Spring: The Politicised Interaction Between Traditional and Alternative Journalistic Practitioners. *Global Media Journal: Australian Edition, 2*(6), 1–13. https://www.hca.westernsydney.edu.au/gmjau/archive/v6_2012_2/pdf/bossio_bebawi_RA_V6-2_2012_GMJAU.pdf. Accessed 20 January 2017.

Boyd-Barrett, O. (2002). Theory in Media Research. In C. Newbold, O. Boyd-Barrett, & H. Van Den Bulck (Eds.), *The Media Book* (pp. 1–54). London: Arnold.

Bunce, M. (2015). Africa in the Click Stream: Audience Metrics and Foreign Correspondents in Africa. *African Journalism Studies, 36*(4), 12–29.

Cooke, R. (2008, April 14). Man of War. *The Guardian*. https://www.theguardian.com/media/2008/apr/13/middleeastthemedia.lebanon. Accessed 16 May 2018.

Cottle, S. (2009). Journalism Studies: Coming of (Global) Age? *Journalism, 10*(3), 309–311.

Couldry, N. (2000). *The Place of Media Power: Pilgrims and Witnesses of the Media Age*. London: Routledge.

Couldry, N., & Curran, J. (2003). The Paradox of Media Power. In N. Couldry & J. Curran (Eds.), *Contesting Media Power: Alternative Media in a Networked World* (pp. 3–15). Oxford: Rowman & Littlefield.

de Burgh, H. (2005). Introduction. In H. de Burgh (Ed.), *Making Journalists: Diverse Models, Global Issues* (pp. 1–21). Florence: Taylor & Francis.

Hamilton, J. M. (2009). *Journalism's Roving Eye: A History of American Foreign Reporting*. Baton Rouge: Louisiana State University Press.

Hamilton, J. M., & Jenner, E. (2004). Redefining Foreign Correspondence. *Journalism, 5*(3), 301–321.

Hamilton, J. M., & Perlmutter, D. D. (2007). *From Pigeons to News Portals: Foreign Reporting and the Challenge of New Technology* (J. M. Hamilton & D. D. Perlmutter, Eds.). Baton Rouge: Louisiana State University Press.

Hannerz, U. (2012). *Foreign News: Exploring the World of Foreign Correspondents.* Chicago: University of Chicago Press.

Herbert, J. (2013). *Practising Global Journalism: Exploring Reporting Issues Worldwide.* New York: Focal Press.

Johnson, T. (2015, March). Desert Storm: The First War Televised Live Around the World (and Around the Clock). *Atlanta Magazine.* http://www.atlantamagazine.com/90s/desert-storm-the-first-war-televised-live-around-the-world-and-around-the-clock/. Accessed 19 April 2018.

Matthews, J. (2013). Journalists and Their Sources: The Twin Challenges of Diversity and Verification. In K. Fowler-Watt & S. Allan (Eds.), *Journalism: New Challenges* (pp. 242–258). Bournemouth: Centre for Journalism & Communication Research, Bournemouth University.

McChesney, R. W. (2003). Corporate Media, Global Capitalism. In S. Cottle (Ed.), *Media Organization and Production* (pp. 27–39). London: Sage.

Mungham, G. (1987). Israel: Fog Over Lebanon. In D. Mercer, G. Mungham, & K. Williams (Eds.), *The Fog of War: The Media on the Battlefield* (pp. 261–290). London: Heinemann.

Murdock, G., & Golding, P. (2005). Culture, Communications and Political Economy. In J. Curran & M. Gurevitch (Eds.), *Mass Media and Society* (4th ed., pp. 60–83). London: Hodder Arnold.

Murrell, C. (2015). *Foreign Correspondents and International Newsgathering: The Role of Fixers.* New York: Routledge.

Rai, M., & Cottle, S. (2007). Global Mediations: On the Changing Ecology of Satellite Television News. *Global Media and Communication, 3*(51), 51–78.

Robinson, P. (2011, April). The CNN Effect Reconsidered: Mapping a Research Agenda for the Future. *Media, War & Conflict, 4*(1), 3–11.

Rogers, J. (2012). *Reporting Conflict.* Hampshire: Palgrave Macmillan.

Sambrook, R. (2010). Are Foreign Correspondents Redundant?: The Changing Face of International News. In *Challenges.* Oxford: Reuters Institute for the Study of Journalism. https://reutersinstitute.politics.ox.ac.uk/sites/default/files/2017-12/Are%20Foreign%20Correspondents%20Redundant%20The%20changing%20face%20of%20international%20news.pdf. Accessed 30 December 2018.

Williams, K. (2011). *International Journalism.* London: Sage.

CHAPTER 4

Reporting Reality

Abstract This chapter argues that without the cultural understanding of the place they are reporting from and the journalistic cultures that exist, foreign correspondents might still not be reporting accurately. The role of the audience is paramount here. What is it modern day audiences are seeking from their journalists, and particularly from foreign correspondents? This chapter argues that it is reality, a true reality understood by the citizens on the ground, not a pre-imagined reality perpetuated for media audiences.

Keywords Foreign correspondent · Fake news · Social reality · Media audiences · Global South Voices · Investigative journalism

Providing an accurate representation of reality in international news is a contentious issue. Historically, foreign correspondents have not necessarily been challenged or held accountable when reporting from remote places, as audiences have taken what they 'witnessed' or reported on as a true account of events. Sambrook (2010) states that 'an unspoken secret of foreign news for many years was that journalists could 'get away' with more because their subjects would never read, see or hear what had been said' (Sambrook 2010: 48). He however points out that this is no longer

© The Author(s) 2019   49
S. Bebawi and M. Evans, *The Future Foreign Correspondent*,
https://doi.org/10.1007/978-3-030-01668-5_4

the case, as the nature of a globalised online environment has meant that interviewees and audiences are aware of what is being reported on and, therefore, can hold foreign reporters accountable—to some extent. Accordingly, Sambrook sees that now more than ever before, foreign correspondents are facing the 'pressure to deliver greater accuracy, fairness and accountability' (Sambrook 2010: 48).

Yet it is important to point out that we mean by reporting reality is not necessarily providing an 'objective' account of the event or issue, but rather offering a portrayal of what is actually happening on the ground by including all aspects of the event. In other words, reporting reality is not journalism that equates different perspectives when there is an imbalance of sides. Reporting reality is about reporting it as it is. CNN foreign correspondent, Christiane Amanpour, talks about this in an interview and illustrates how reality is reported in conflict through her experience with the Bosnian War from 1992 to 1996. She stresses that 'calling it as it is' is not biased reporting and is not 'taking sides'. She states:

> Objectivity I believe means giving each side their hearing but not treating each side the same, not drawing a moral equivalence which would be a false equivalence. Not saying 'on the one hand, on the other hand'. The person who's being sniped and killed is somehow equal to the person who's sniping and killing. The forces who are bombarding, besieging and shelling a city full of civilians do not have the same moral standing as those who are being bombed, shelled, starved and besieged. And that is the truth, that was the truth that we found and that we reported, and that to this day set the standard certainly for myself and my generation of how we report, how we tell the stories, when we're faced with these severe situations. (Amanpour 2012)

Often reporters might think they are reporting the truth, however without the cultural understanding of the place they are reporting on and the journalistic cultures that exist within that place, foreign correspondents might still not be reporting accurately. This chapter will discuss these different scenarios and situations which is particularly important with the rise of fake news in the current media environment. It is central to note, however, that it is not within the scope of this chapter to discuss truth-telling and journalism, instead what we are concerned with here is how reality does or does not get reported on by foreign correspondents, with a focus on the factors that make it improbable to do so.

NEWS AND THE CONSTRUCTION OF REALITY

In order to consider how foreign correspondents report reality, there is first a need to distinguish 'reality' from the construction of reality. Nick Couldry and Andreas Hepp (2017) see that the facts that define reality are static, however it is the construction of that reality that varies. They argue that there is 'one physical world, but many possible, and even conflicting, constructions of it' (Couldry and Hepp 2017: 22). Within a global context of events, foreign correspondents play a crucial role in the construction of this reality especially since they are often the only ones who have access to that reality within the mediated global sphere. Brian McNair states that 'journalism is not and never could be reality in the first, absolute sense. It can be, at best, only a version of reality, constructed according to rules, codes and conventions which we associate with journalistic discourse' (McNair 2005: 30). Yet an underlying question remains: where is reality situated within these various constructions of events? Even more importantly, which of these constructions is in fact closer to a more holistic representation?

In his book *The Myth of Media Globalization*, Kai Hafez (2007) argues that most media content, through international reporting, is 'lost in translation when news is transferred from one media system to another' (2007: 25). He states that '[m]edia content is distorted whenever international reporting more strongly reflects the national interests and cultural stereotypes of the *reporting* country than the news reality of the country *being reported about*' (Hafez 2007: 25). He continues to state that this is mainly due to media concentrating on national markets and audiences, 'whose interests and stereotypes they largely reproduce' (Hafez 2007: 25). This is one reason reality gets distorted in international reporting: the concentration on local markets and national audiences means that news content and angles will be structured to cater for that, thus omitting other aspects of the event or story.

Oliver Boyd-Barrett (2002) explains how the media construct a particular reality, through what he outlines as the process by which the media 'portray, reflect, filter and negotiate the 'real world', such that 'our ways of knowing that world, is influenced by the media and by widespread assumptions about the power of the media' (Boyd-Barrett 2002: 16). This, he suggests, is achieved through the media's construction of the world through a process of 'selection, exclusion and inclusion', which leads to media channels offering particular versions of reality. Consequently, as a result of this 'selection, exclusion and inclusion', the media have the ability to reduce or redraw the boundaries of actual reality and set the limits accordingly. These limits become the parameters through which our understanding of the world takes place.

The role the media play in selecting and defining the news, in turn defines what is labelled as 'social reality'. Social reality reflects society's set of beliefs and values. According to Couldry (2003) dominant media not only reflect the news discourses which appeal to the majority of audiences, but also enforce the views and perspectives which appeal to the dominant media, thus providing a cyclical enforcement of that reality. This process is what Couldry labels as 'media rituals', whereby 'any actions organised around key media-related categories and boundaries, whose performance reinforces, indeed helps legitimate, the underlying 'value' expressed in the idea that the media is our access point to our social centre' (Couldry 2003: 2). Hence the construction of social reality, according to Couldry, is intrinsically a 'social process' where media power acts as a reproduction of the 'social practice' of its audience members. This is achieved by the media's 'circulation of images and discourse' that reproduce what is embedded in social practice. Foreign correspondents are trained to do this and, consequently practice it—knowingly or unknowingly. They are trained to focus on their audience in the construction of the media message rather than focus on relaying what is happening on the ground. This is not to say that they are misleading their audiences, rather that they are trained to tailor news discourses to appeal to their national audiences. Editors are continuously asking foreign correspondents to relate stories back to what is of interest to their audiences. Consequently, what the media produce is not 'something superimposed on social practice from the outside; instead it is endlessly reproduced through the details of social practice itself' (Couldry 2000: 5). This leads to the reproduction of, what Couldry labels as, society's 'local patterns of belief' (Couldry 2000: 5) where, by mirroring the discourses of their local social context, the media make these discourses 'natural' to their audience.

Although it is also not realistic for foreign correspondents to tell all aspects of an event and cover all the issues involved, news is formatted in a way that takes on the shape of conventional and tested discourses, and which are known to appeal to the majority of audiences, and in turn shape society's systems of beliefs. The role the media therefore play in selecting and defining the news, in turn, defines social reality.

Constant images always portraying other countries as 'foreign' could only lead to increasing and emphasising the cultural gap of understanding. The 'other' (Said 1978) becomes distant, and in turn attitudes and policies are shaped accordingly. This of course, cannot be blamed solely on the foreign correspondent, however it is important not to undermine the influence that international reporting has on the shaping of these views globally. On this basis, it is essential that foreign correspondents play a conscious role in working outside conventional discourses that assist in understanding and connecting with the 'other'. Constant portrayals of Africans as poor and hungry or refugees in the Middle East as helpless, although true images, are one side of reality. Such constant portrayals fail to also outline the commonalities shared across cultures, and in turn reveal other aspects of reality.

What Audiences Want

The above section discussed how reality is shaped in line with society's set of beliefs. However, other factors have also played a role in forcing foreign reporting to cater for national audiences that does not necessarily reflect an accurate representation of reality. The effect of financial constraints and limitations on international reporting has led to cutbacks on the employment of foreign correspondents, thus shaping what local audiences are exposed to and in turn are interested in. Williams (2011: 94–95) talks about how there has been a decline in interest in international news by local audiences due to cut backs in budgets by major news organisations since the 1980s, and which is mainly due to the deregulation of US television and the need to rely on market forces. However, Williams notes that this is an American explanation due to research focusing on the American media environments, yet these reasons can still be regarded as effective factors across the world due to the domination of the US industries on the global news market.

The reason behind the lack of interest by audiences in news from other countries can also be traced back to audiences not relating to the areas, people and issues reported on. In turn, as we argue in the following chapter, there is a need for foreign correspondents to make those connections through their reporting that create cultural bridging and awareness that would ideally lead to building a more informed and engaged global community. Sambrook (2010) notes the existence of gaps in international reporting between different cultures around the world, inherently arguing that this gap is due to local audiences being more interested in local issues rather than global ones. This leads national broadcasters and newspapers to prioritise the coverage of local events rather than global ones. He expands on this:

> The need to explain the interdependence of the world grows, but cultural gulfs are still wide and most audiences are more interested in local issues than global ones. The role of cultural bridge is of growing not lessening importance and cannot always be achieved by indigenous reporters. For all the virtues of employing local staff for an informed local perspective, the outsider's view remains essential too. Distance provides perspective. (Sambrook 2010: 53)

Sambrook however points out that audiences are more complex and cannot just be identified as 'local', since journalists are dealing with a more global and shuffling audience, where we see Australians living in the UK watching their local broadcaster online, the Australian Broadcasting Service (ABC), doing so with a UK perspective. This is due to audiences having what Sambrook labels as 'bilateral identities' (Sambrook 2010: 53), or multiple identities for that matter. Communities are shifting from being exclusively local geographically to becoming communities of interest. This resonates with what Jarvis (2014) says, noting that it is absolutely vital that journalists (students too) find the community for their reporting. The global audience referred to below is attracted to communities of interest—in one sense it is why the Zumba story from FCST experience, see Chapter 6, worked. Williams notes that global journalism is meant for 'global' interests: 'In transcending national boundaries, people are demanding an international journalism that is more 'global' in content and approach. Transnationalisation is bringing about a global audience for news' (Williams 2011: 163). Accordingly, foreign correspondents attempting to cater and shape their news discourses according to a specific local audience, find it increasingly hard in the current media environment. For this reason, a global humanistic outlook to news production could yield better results in terms of bridging cultural gaps around the world and providing a more representative account of reality. If done correctly, such journalism could highlight the commonalities and normalise the 'other' as opposed to the traditional notion of foreign reporting as 'telling stories from far away lands'.

In a study of slant in US newspapers, Matthew Gentzkow and Je M. Shapiro (2010) found that readers tend to confirm news that matches their ideological preferences, for what they call 'like-minded news' (Gentzkow and Shapiro 2010: 35), thus confirming Couldry's argument earlier. They sum up their findings as follows:

> While we do not have direct evidence on the institutional mechanism through which newspapers "choose" their slant, the choice of editorial staff (along with choice of topics and explicit style policies) seems like a plausible channel through which newspaper content is calibrated to the views of the local population. (Gentzkow and Shapiro 2010: 64)

Yet there is a different school of thought that sees that it is the audiences that seek news outlets that comply to their beliefs, under which Raymond S. Nickerson (1998) labelled as 'conformation bias'. Through 'conformation bias', 'readers seek out and more readily believe information conforming to prior beliefs' (quoted in Casey and Owen 2013: 295), where audiences 'listen to news commentators who interpret current events in a way that they like' (Nickerson 1998: 199), and this doesn't seem to have changed.

Whether it is the editors who follow their audiences, or audiences who follow their news outlets, reporting reality seems to be at stake here especially when it comes to knowing and learning about events and people from other parts of the world who are not within our line of sight. Hannerz (2012) argues that our knowledge of the world is largely shaped by foreign news reporting, which in turn places a 'burden' on media organisations. He explains:

> Any feeling we may have of being at home in the world, away from our most immediate, routine habitat, is thus likely to be quite unevenly distributed. There are regions for which that wider embeddedness of news reporting in knowledge of some other derivation may be strong, and others for which it is weak. In the latter case, what we know, or believe we know, will in unusually large part be based on what we read, or hear, or see, as media consumers. And the burden on media reporting to shape the world images of audiences then becomes especially heavy. Whether it is a burden it can cope with will in turn depend in no small part on the way media organizations arrange their own commitments in time and space. (Hannerz 2012: 37–38)

...ut that based on regions of the world that media
...n, audiences develop 'weak' and 'strong' knowledge
...of the world. So not only is it necessary for foreign
...ge the knowledge gap on particular countries of inter-
...is essential for reporters to expand their reporting beyond
of the world that commonly make the world news agenda.
...ital requirement when it comes to expanding the boundaries
o. ...nce's social reality, as daily news plays a role in dictating *which*
coun...ies we know about and *what* we know about them. Consequently,
if there are parts of the world which become absent in global reporting,
then their existence to a global audience is also absent.

In short, the role of the foreign correspondent essentially needs to
be that of global story-telling for a global audience, with global interests. This is not to say that foreign correspondents can always offer every
aspect and angle of 'reality' since reporters often have very limited time
to do so, however the inclusion of a variety of discourses within their
reporting that address the knowledge gap is what is necessary.

Voices from the Global South

In the 1980 UNESCO report, *Many Voices One World: Towards a New
More Just and More Efficient World Information and Communication
Order*—or what came to be widely referred to as the MacBride report,
concerns were raised regarding the distortion of news content globally
at the time. The report found that generally the public was not well
informed, to the extent that the report noted that 'many public or private bodies may also be ill-informed, uninformed or, more serious still,
misinformed or misled', and this is due to the distortion of content
where there were widespread 'inaccuracies and deficiencies in the circulation of news' (UNESCO 1980: 156). This has not changed, as international reporting practices have also not changed, as discussed thus
far. This, in fact, has been further complicated with the rise in fake news
where there has been an increase of unverified content, as we discuss
later in this chapter.

Nonetheless, the field of international news has witnessed the entry
of non-Western global broadcasters seeking to both counter-balance
and compete with Western 24-hour news channels. In South America,
there are fewer news channels than North America but there are some
prominent satellite television stations such as the Brazilian *Globonews*,

Argentina's *Todo Noticias* and Venezuela's *Telesur* Network. Throughout South Asia, Rai and Cottle (2007) note a domination of Indian media, however, in East Asia, Taiwan is a media centre alongside significant broadcasters such as China's English *CCTV-9*, Hong Kong's *Phoenix News*, and Singapore's *Channel News Asia*. As for the Middle East, *Al Jazeera* has been expanding its reach through its English language satellite channel. Africa is also a region of marked silence, yet the *South Africa Broadcasting Cooperation* (*SABC*) has been influential. Local foreign correspondents working for these news organisations are now reporting side by side with Western reporters on world issues for their local audiences, including reporting to global audiences. So the image of the typical Western reporter standing in front of the camera and reporting on the developing world, has now been reversed by the rise of reporters from the global South reporting on Western and non-Western countries. This provides an opportunity for regions from the global South to counter news discourses and offer a different perspective or position to dominant Western narratives, not only on their countries but also on world events and issues. Ultimately, what this allows for is the clarification and expansion of the discursive transcultural sphere. However whether this means that a more accurate representation of reality would emerge or not, has yet to be tested. Nonetheless, the widening of the discursive news sphere to allow for different perspectives from various regions of the world would certainly be expected.

One form of journalism that lies at the core of fact checking and evidence-based reporting is investigative journalism. There have been numerous examples, some of which we will discuss here, of foreign correspondents working with local investigative journalists and which have proven to be successful. This relates to discussions made in the previous chapter on how foreign correspondents could benefit from jointly working with local reporters, thus addressing challenges which would have risen had each of them worked independently. Working with local investigative journalists also addresses the time limits that foreign correspondents have, as local investigative reporters tend to have more time on the ground to work on researching, investigating and evidencing the story on an in-depth level.

There has been a rise of investigative reporting in the developing world, especially conflict-ridden countries, at a time when this form of journalism has been diminishing in the Western world due mainly to economic constraints. Regions of the global South, such as Africa, Asia, and the Middle East have witnessed a rise in training organisations for investigative journalism, and in turn the emergence of investigative stories that often have led to some form of social or political change. Investigative journalism is regarded as a form of journalism that informs the public about something that is of importance to them and which they do not know about (Aucoin 2006). This role is similar to what we argue foreign correspondence should be doing—that is informing the global audience of news that they do not know about, outside repeated and tried discourses that do little to enhance and expand global knowledge. Although this is one way through which foreign correspondents can provide accurate fact-checked journalism, it is an effective way in which foreign reporters can achieve in-depth news stories that encompass an accurate reporting of reality.

A successful example of how investigative reporters have worked with foreign reporters is an investigative story entitled *Jordan's Secret Shame*, which was conducted in collaboration with the BBC (Bebawi 2016). This story aimed to uncover the maltreatment, negligence, and daily abuse of children with physical and mental disabilities in private care homes for children. The local investigative reporter, Hanan Khandakji, posed as a volunteer worker in these homes and documented beatings and abuse of children over a period of time. Both this role and the time it took to collect all the evidence is something that cannot be achieved by a foreign correspondent alone. Once the story was aired on the BBC, the investigation sparked noise at an international and local Jordanian level. As a result of this story being aired on BBC, a Jordanian committee was set up to look into the claims of maltreatment in children's care homes across Jordan, and within two weeks it submitted its final report supporting the findings of the collaborative investigative story. In response to the committee report, the governments closed down three centres, and eight private care homes faced allegations of abuse where several caseworkers faced criminal charges (Allen, 23 January 2013). In addition, 'Jordan's government promised to revise policies and laws to meet international human rights standards' (Allen, 23 January 2013). Khandakji regarded the collaboration with foreign BBC reporters as vital to the success of the story, where she notes that '[i]f the same report come out in local media, it won't have the same affect. [Jordanian authorities] are afraid of the international scandal' (Allen, 23 January 2013). In addition, the BBC journalists offered their expertise and advice on how to investigate the story, so in essence it was useful for both the local and foreign reporter. This story is an example of how investigative journalism can be a powerful tool for change in the developing world when done in collaboration with international reporters, who have the journalistic skills and expertise, the international platform with the global reach, and who generally also have the immunity as international reporters.

Depending on where foreign correspondents report from, their freedom is restricted and this needs to be acknowledged. William A. Hachten and James F. Scotton (2007) note that '[a] foreign correspondent often defines a country as free or not free according to how much difficulty he or she has in reporting events there' (Hachten and Scotton 2007: 131). They also note that although this sounds 'narrow and self-serving', it is true to some extent, especially when local journalists themselves have limited freedom to do their journalism (Hachten and Scotton 2007: 131). Yet there are ways to go around this, as we note through another example of how foreign correspondents can assist local reporters to get stories accessible to a global audience through their privilege of immunity. One example is a story where investigative reporters in the Philippines worked in collaboration with foreign correspondents from Reuters on the local drug war in 2016, and as a result a series of stories came out in international media. Howie Severino, who is a prominent investigative reporter from the Philippines, talks about how foreign correspondents work with local investigative reporters who are not able to report or publish certain stories as they fear for their safety. As a result stories get published by the foreign correspondents after they have left the country. Howie explains:

> Why is it that it's mostly the foreign journalists coming and doing this kind of digging but notice that a lot of this reportage comes out when these foreign journalists are gone. They come, they stay for like weeks, they got all this information, they take all these photos, they take all these videos, they do great stuff, they go back to their home country, or their home office, package all of this, put it in online, put in on TV or whatever, creates an impact. You see if a Filipino did that, his life would be in danger. (Howie, 12 December 2016)

Howie goes on to clarify this is in fact done with the help of local investigative reporters, and explains why they do this:

What we do is that we help these people out. They get the credit and all that, but hey, that's not why we're doing this. We want the information out […] we're all in this together. (Howie, 12 December 2016)

Such collaborations between foreign correspondents and local investigative reporters can result in strong journalism that is mutually beneficial: the foreign correspondent gets to report on an in-depth and accurate story that addresses his or her limitations of time, access to information and local knowledge; and the local investigative reporter is guaranteed that their story gets published, reaching an international audience, and having their voices included in a global media sphere. This collaboration therefore could address some of the issues for both parties. Yet this is only one specific form of journalism, and one that does not address the daily reporting of events or breaking news.

REALITY IN A 'FAKE NEWS' ENVIRONMENT

Reporting reality has become an issue of concern with the rise of 'fake news'. The previous chapter highlighted some challenges to international reporting, such as parachute journalism and citizen journalism, which impede the foreign correspondent's ability to report reality despite their best intentions to do so. Hence difficulties in reporting reality are not new, as accurate representations have always been a challenge in international reporting. This becomes particularly difficult in an environment of fake news reporting. Definitions of fake news tend to be unclear, however according to the 2017 *Reuters Institute Digital News Report*, fake news is defined through three categories: '(1) news that is 'invented' to make money or discredit others; (2) news that has a basis in fact, but is 'spun' to suit a particular agenda; and (3) news that people don't feel comfortable about or don't agree with' (Newman et al. 2017: 19). From this definition, the second category relates to how news is constructed to fit particular news agendas, and the third category relates to how audiences follow news that fits their own agenda.

In an article entitled *Escape from Reality*, Laurie Penny makes a notable point stating that '[f]ake news sells because fake news is what people want to be true. Fake news generates clicks because people click on things that they want to believe' (Penny 2017: 18). This relates to the arguments made in this chapter on the media having to cater for audience needs. Audiences have always consumed news that fits with their beliefs and rejected news that doesn't, yet in an environment where fake news is becoming more prevalent this makes the work of foreign correspondents not only difficult but also crucial in get the reality right. In a study conducted by Dominik Stecula (2017), it was found that audiences cannot identify the difference between fake news and actual news. He believes the reason behind this is because 'the public might not be well-equipped to separate quality information from false information' (Stecula 2017).

Fake news is not new. Brian McNair states that 'information – or misinformation – has always been an important weapon of ideological warfare, and fake news can be seen as one particular form of a more generally utilised battery of information warfare tools' (McNair 2017: 23). However, foreign correspondents reporting conflict in today's environment of fake news face a larger challenge than ever before, which means that they have a more important role to play. Through a study of a British foreign correspondents, Cristina Archetti (2012) challenges the assumption that foreign correspondents are bound to disappear, and instead argues that they have a major role to play as 'sense makers', especially in a digital environment that offers an abundance of information and fake news. Archetti notes that '[w]hile foreign journalists have to a large extent always fulfilled this function, they appear more needed than ever in a deeply interdependent world' (Archetti 2012: 847).

In an era where fake news is widespread and there is an abundance of information, foreign correspondents have a more vital role to play than ever before. Their closeness to events on the ground, along with their ability to clarify and bridge different cultural discourses makes their presence necessary as fact checkers and communicators of 'reality'. The issues discussed in this chapter on reporting reality, provide an emphasised responsibility upon foreign correspondents to relay an accurate representation of reality, especially when reporting within transcultural spheres. The following chapter will discuss this further.

References

Allen, B. (2013, January 23). A Brave Young Journalist in Jordan. *Journalists for Human Rights.* http://www.jhr.ca/blog/2013/01/a-brave-young-journalists-in-jordan/. Accessed 5 December 2014.

Amanpour, C. (2012). *Objectivity in War.* https://www.youtube.com/watch?v=tqwYyAzux6M. Accessed 14 May 2018.

Archetti, C. (2012). Which Future for Foreign Correspondence?: London Foreign Correspondents in the Age of Global Media. *Journalism Studies, 13*(5–6), 847–856.

Aucoin, J. (2006). *The Evolution of American Investigative Journalism.* Columbia: University of Missouri Press.

Bebawi, S. (2016). *Investigative Journalism in the Arab World: Issues and Challenges.* London: Palgrave.

Boyd-Barrett, O. (2002). Theory in Media Research. In C. Newbold, O. Boyd-Barrett, & H. Van Den Bulck (Eds.), *The Media Book* (pp. 1–54). London: Arnold.

Casey, G. P., & Owen, A. L. (2013). Good News, Bad News, and Consumer Confidence. *Social Science Quarterly, 94*(1), 292–315.

Couldry, N. (2000). *The Place of Media Power: Pilgrims and Witnesses of the Media Age.* London: Routledge.

Couldry, N. (2003). Beyond the Hall of Mirrors? Some Theoretical Reflections on the Global Contestation of Media Power. In N. Couldry & J. Curran (Eds.), *Contesting Media Power: Alternative Media in a Networked World* (pp. 39–54). Oxford: Rowman & Littlefield.

Couldry, N., & Hepp, A. (2017). *The Mediated Construction of Reality.* Cambridge: Polity Press.

Gentzkow, M., & Shapiro, J. M. (2010). What Drives Media Slant? Evidence from U.S. Daily Newspapers. *Econometrica, 78*(1), 35–71.

Hachten, W. A., & Scotton, J. F. (2007). *The World News Prism: Global Information in a Satellite Age.* Oxford: Blackwell Publishing.

Hafez, K. (2007). *The Myth of Media Globalization.* Cambridge: Polity Press.

Hannerz, U. (2012). *Foreign News: Exploring the World of Foreign Correspondents.* Chicago: University of Chicago Press.

Howie, S. (2016, December 12). Interview with Saba Bebawi. *Vice President for Professional Development at GMA Network.* Manila, Philippines.

Jarvis, J. (2014). *Geeks Bearing Gifts: Imagining New Futures for News.* New York: CUNY Journalism Press.

McNair, B. (2005). Introduction. In G. Issues & H. de Burgh (Eds.), *Making Journalists: Diverse Models* (pp. 25–43). Florence: Taylor & Francis.

McNair, B. (2017). *Fake News: Falsehood, Fabrication and Fantasy in Journalism.* New York: Routledge.

Newman, N., Fletcher, R., Kalogeropoulos, A., Levy, D. A. L., & Nielsen, R. K. (2017). *Reuters Institute Digital News Report 2017.* Reuters Institute for the Study of Journalism. https://reutersinstitute.politics.ox.ac.uk/sites/default/files/Digital%20News%20Report%202017%20web_0.pdf?utm_source=digitalnewsreport.org&utm_medium=referral. Accessed 16 May 2018.

Nickerson, R. S. (1998). Confirmation Bias: A Ubiquitous Phenomenon in Many Guises. *Review of General Psychology, 2*(2), 175–220.

Penny, L. (2017, January 20–26). Escape from Reality: Fake News Sells Because People Want It to Be True. *New Statesman*, 18–19.

Rai, M., & Cottle, S. (2007). Global Mediations: On the Changing Ecology of Satellite Television News. *Global Media and Communication*, 3(51), 51–78.

Said, E. (1978). *Orientalism*. London: Routledge & Kegan Paul.

Sambrook, R. (2010). Are Foreign Correspondents Redundant?: The Changing Face of International News. In *Challenges*. Oxford: Reuters Institute for the Study of Journalism. https://reutersinstitute.politics.ox.ac.uk/sites/default/files/2017-12/Are%20Foreign%20Correspondents%20Redundant%20The%20changing%20face%20of%20international%20news.pdf. Accessed 30 December 2017.

Stecula, D. (2017, July 27). The Real Consequences of Fake News. *The Conversation*. https://theconversation.com/the-real-consequences-of-fake-news-81179. Accessed 28 May 2018.

UNESCO Report by the International Commission for the Study of Communication Problems. (1980). *Communication and Society Today and Tomorrow, Many Voices One World: Towards a New More Just and More Efficient World Information and Communication Order*. London: Kogan Page; New York: Unipub; Paris: UNESCO.

Williams, K. (2011). *International Journalism*. London: Sage.

CHAPTER 5

Transcultural Spheres
and the Foreign Correspondent

Abstract This chapter looks into the need for being aware of the existence of various journalism cultures, as many studies have showcased. A cultural understanding of the place journalists report from is a complex matter, and many factors need to be taken into consideration, such as social, political, economic, religious and historic ones. This chapter focuses on two axis that intersect: The first considers the pre-existing cultures that any journalist consciously or unconsciously brings to bear on their subject. The second analyses how that understanding in turn affects the cultural discourse that their journalism produces and the extent to which it can assist in developing transcultural spheres.

Keywords Foreign correspondent · Cultures of journalism ·
Transcultural spheres · Parachute journalism · Cultural news discourse ·
Happy news

Acquiring a cultural understanding of the place that is reported from is a complex matter, and many factors need to be taken into consideration to ensure an accurate representation of reality. These factors are seen as social, political, economic, religious and historic factors that shape news discourses within transcultural spheres. This chapter will discuss the complexities of reporting within transcultural spheres, arguing that in an online environment, foreign correspondents can play a major role that distinguishes their journalism from other sources such as citizen

© The Author(s) 2019
S. Bebawi and M. Evans, *The Future Foreign Correspondent*,
https://doi.org/10.1007/978-3-030-01668-5_5

reporting or online news, which as discussed, are regarded as threats to their trade. Repetitive and continuous standardised images of different parts of the 'foreign' world have tended to not only neutralise the impact of an event or people, but also deliver a message that this is the only way these 'other' people live—a message that continues to confirm their 'foreignness', since their issues, problems and way of life are very remote to that of the target audience. This leads to questions such as: Why don't foreign correspondents challenge this message? Why don't they provide a transcultural lens to their reporting, and in turn articulate connections between the country being reported on and their audiences? And why don't they tell the happy positive stories of different countries and people? This chapter touches on these questions.

According to Williams (2011) negative reporting has 'particular implications for the coverage of Africa, Asia and Latin America, which has for many periods in the post-war years been reported on TV news in terms of violence and disorder' (Williams 2011: 108). This has implications and in turn impacts views on racism, tourism, social ties, and political understandings. Williams argues that:

> The failure of western journalism and diplomacy to comprehend and interpret the Third World stems from an in-built, historical set of assumptions of these countries and their relations with the West. There is a limited realisation of how their own cultural background shapes their understanding of events in other cultures. (Williams 2011: 108)

There are therefore two cultural axis to consider here when looking into the role of the foreign correspondent communicating within transcultural spheres: the first is related to the culture of journalism that the reporter comes from and uses, and the second is the extent to which he/she is aware of various factors that play a role in the culture of journalism within the country reported on. This in turn affects the cultural discourse that is adopted in their reporting and the extent to which it can assist in developing transcultural spheres. In essence, therefore, the first axis relates to the *practice of journalism* itself, and the second relates to how the practice consequently affects the *discursive outcome*.

These are both important aspects that affect the role of the foreign correspondent in shaping and developing transcultural spheres of understanding. The need for foreign correspondents to be aware of the factors that shape different cultures of journalism is tied to training reporters to be aware of this, and is also tied to how it manifests in their news discourses. This chapter will discuss both these aspects by first looking into the key factors that play a role in the culture of journalism, and then by exploring the importance of cultural connections to be established through the notion of 'happy news' or the positive framing of discursive news output. First, however, there is a need to understand what is meant by transcultural spheres in international reporting.

REPORTING TRANSCULTURAL SPHERES

Cultural representations not only occur through one discursive sphere, but are expressed through the overlapping of more than one sphere across borders through transcultural spheres. Transcultural spheres refer to the complex and overlayed articulation of varied public spheres (Hepp 2015: 167). Foreign correspondents can act as a conduit of knowledge through transcultural spheres, however according to Barbie Zelizer, they are not only seen as 'conveyors of information but also as producers of culture' (Zelizer 2005: 200). In the previous chapter we discussed how, in an environment of fake news, foreign correspondents need to report on reality as accurately as possible and one way of doing this is through bridging cultural gaps, which include social, political, and historic nuances. John O'Regan and Malcolm MacDonald (2007) believe that this can be achieved through what they see as an interventionist role that intercultural communication can play. They explain that as:

> The discourse of intercultural communication, for that is what we shall call it, seeks to be interventionist and prefers to think of itself as such [...] It intervenes in the transnational public arena of intercultural debate in the belief that such interventions may help to reduce conflict, promote cooperation and increase intercultural understanding. (O'Regan and MacDonald 2007: 268)

This is of course an optimistic notion of what intercultural communication can achieve, as in reality there are many challenges to this. According to the UNESCO (2009) report on *Investing in Cultural Diversity and Intercultural Dialogue*, there are three reasons that can be attributed to the persistence of dominant cultural representations in news media over others, and these are: (1) mass media tend to repeat and reinforce the 'longevity of these representations'; (2) media tend to be profit-driven and hence favour introducing simple representations which undermine problematic ones; (3) and finally, the media tend to be aligned closely with elites and thus would avoid 'changing the status quo' (UNESCO 2009: 141). For these reasons foreign correspondents need to play a crucial role in challenging the persistence of these cultural representations, which can be enforced through their training and practice.

Williams (2011), however, outlines a few reasons as to why foreign correspondents have not traditionally played this role, one of which is due to the 'relatively little relevant knowledge or skills related to the area or region to which they are assigned', and by the time reporters starts to gain an understanding of the local culture and language they are then assigned to another part of the world (Williams 2011: 98). Having said this, he points out that a firm grasp of the local culture and language can often eschew their reporting and affect their ability to provide a balanced view. He states that:

> Rapid rotation has become a feature of the way in which western news organisations deal with foreign assignments: there is an assumption that 'going stale' or 'going native' is an occupational hazard. (Williams 2011: 99)

Williams speaks of the 'generalist approach' that foreign correspondents have been encouraged to adopt, meaning that 'generalists are able to represent more effectively their audience, seeing the world through their eyes, which specialist knowledge might impede', in addition to the fact that specialist knowledge is 'a costly and time-consuming activity' (Williams 2011: 100). He states:

> A sceptical attitude to specialist knowledge and skills is deeply ingrained in the occupational culture of international journalism, which has come to place considerable emphasis on the 'generalist'. He or she is supposed to represent the audience they are reporting for – which usually means in foreign coverage an audience that is often unaware. Speaking to them is as important, if not more important, than getting the story right. (Williams 2011: 98)

The NWICO report states that '[t]he media have the power to promote public awareness and understanding of the culture, the social habits and traditions, the attitudes and hopes — and also the grievances — of each diverse group in the population', and based on that the report called for 'journalists to be trained in a way that enables them to play their part more effectively in this area' (UNESCO 1980: 188). Yet a cultural understanding of the place journalists report from is a complex matter, and many factors need to be taken into consideration. This following section will discuss these factors in relation to the foreign correspondent through Reese's (2001) *Hierarchy of Influences* model for global journalists, stressing the need for reporters to be trained to operate and navigate transcultural spheres with the aim of greater cultural diversity and representation.

CULTURES OF JOURNALISM

As noted above, we see that reporting within transcultural spheres occurs through two axis: the first is the process, and this pertains to how different cultures do journalism differently and, in turn, how it affects the news discourse; and the second axis is the outcome, which we discuss in the following section by focusing on how intercultural connections could be developed through news discourses that provide positive news. This section will look into these different factors that make up cultures of journalism.

According to Stephen D. Reese, many journalism scholars hold the belief that 'there should be an international standard of journalistic professionalism with basic shared values' (Reese 2001: 173). Yet there are others who believe that a universal 'way' of doing journalism does not take into consideration the varying cultural factors that play a role in the construction of news. So although there is somewhat 'an all-encompassing consensus among journalists toward a common understanding and cultural identity of journalism', there are, however, different 'professional ideologies' which are practiced through varying journalism cultures (Hanitzsch 2007: 368) and, in turn, reflect a variety of journalistic practices. The contexts differ, and therefore to assume that what has traditionally been known to be a 'universal' or 'Western' way of doing journalism is not realistic. It is problematic when a foreign correspondent reporting from another country, therefore, does not take into account the different cultural considerations, social expectations, or even historical narratives that usually sit outside Western perceptions and which make up the local culture of journalism.

According to the *Worlds of Journalism Study*, there are key variables that shape a country's journalism culture, and they include the socio-demographic backgrounds; journalists in the newsroom; editorial autonomy; perceived influences; journalistic roles; ethical orientations; reporting practices; perceived change; and institutional trust (Worlds of Journalism 2012–2016). However, Reese's (2001) *Hierarchy of Influences* model assists in providing a framework that helps understand the factors that influence the reporting culture of the global journalist, and which we will discuss in some detail here. What is useful about this model is that it considers the influencers and factors that play a role in shaping news from the micro to macro level. Hence what the Hierarchy of Influences model for the study of global journalism does is it 'proposes important distinctions between levels of analysis and locates the individual journalist within a web of organizational and ideological constraints' (Reese 2001: 174). Understanding the varying macro and micro levels of influences on global journalists would therefore allow us to unpack the intricacies of how foreign correspondents produce global journalism, and what different factors international reporters need to take into consideration when operating within a transcultural sphere, communicating across borders and to varying audiences around the world.

Reese states that 'this model requires that we take into account the larger structure within which these journalists function' (Reese 2001: 173). What this model allows for, therefore, is a 'sociology-of media view, which considers how media power functions within a larger social context' (Reese 2001: 174). Although Reese recommends using this model for comparative research, the different influences are particularly useful in an abstract understanding of journalism within transcultural spheres. Reese (2001) points out that 'the interesting question may be not how professional one country's journalists are compared with another's, but how professionalism comes to mean something different in different cultures' (Reese 2001: 178) and, in turn, how foreign correspondents navigate different journalism cultures in their reporting.

According to Reese (2001), the Hierarchy of Influences are situated within each other to shape media content, starting at a micro level with the individual level, which relates to the 'attitudes, training, and background of the journalist' (Reese 2001: 179). The journalist himself or herself play an influential role in the shaping of a media message, despite it being at the micro level. This level can influence the media content for various reasons. One is deeply connected to how journalists perceive their roles to be (Deuze 2002; Hanitzsch 2017). The culture of journalism that the foreign correspondent comes from, therefore, also plays an important role. In a study that aimed to understanding the discursive news output of AJE, it was found that Western reporters tended to provide a different and often even a contradicting discourse to Arab reporters coming out of the same newsroom and reporting on the same event (Bebawi 2016). This evidently places emphasis on how the culture of journalism that the reporter comes from, that is shaped by their training, journalistic experiences, audiences they report to, and even their own social backgrounds, can drastically change the perceptive lens through which a news discourse is constructed. When a foreign correspondent reports on an event in another country, they will do so through their individual level thus drastically changing social reality. Consequently, it can be argued that if foreign correspondents were to be aware of the different local journalism cultures they are reporting from and take them into account when reporting, then this could allow for a more representative discursive output of the place they are reporting.

The next level of hierarchy in Reese's model is the *routines model*, where he points out that 'individuals do not have complete freedom to act on their beliefs and attitudes, but must operate within a multitude of limits imposed by technology, time, space, and norms' (Reese 2001: 180). It is precisely these 'norms' and ways of doing things that provide a cultural practice of journalism at the routines level. Although the routines influences are outside the control of the reporter, Reese makes the point that 'we assume that much of what journalists provide as reasons for their behavior are actually justifications for what they have already been obliged to do by forces outside their control' (Reese 2001: 181). In other words, the routines influence has become intrinsic in the culture of journalism for journalists at an individual level. Foreign correspondents, therefore, operate within the realm of the influences level as part of their daily reporting.

Influences from an *organizational level* dictate how '[e]ditorial policy, in particular, allows the organization to shape what stories are considered newsworthy, how they are prioritized, and how they are framed' (Reese 2001: 181). In turn, from a political economy perspective, the news agenda of the global journalist is very much dictated by what his or her organisation deems as important to report on and what is not. This is a crucial point when reporting within transcultural spheres, as it shapes which news discourse s are to be included and which are not. This lies in the heart of how foreign correspondents report on news. The issue here, however, is that often international reporters have little control over how they can shape their media message. Arguably, however, if foreign correspondents continue to operate within safe and tested frames, their ability to provide different and challenging discourses becomes limited. Foreign correspondents, therefore, can be seen as strong advocates for changing global news discourses due to their proximity to events on the ground despite their organisational and editorial restrictions.

However, at an *extra-media level*, influences sit outside the organisation, and are therefore positioned outside the control of the foreign correspondent all together. Such influences include other organisations, government bodies, influential sources, advertisers, and interest groups. The use of sources here are a crucial component to foreign correspondents, as access to sources could assist in communicating the reality on the ground despite these extra-media level influences. If foreign reporters are trained to access sources that provide in-depth and varying accounts, then the news story is constructed to reflect varying perspectives and discourses. Traditionally, foreign correspondents have referred to the same sources that have been used by other reporters, such as political commentators or the same organisations, as these are sources that are not only accessible but also are tried. Time limitations are often a reason for why foreign correspondents end up using the same sources, and this could also be due to using the same fixers, yet the insistence on behalf of reporters to use and provide perspectives from different sources is an essential element to the development of a more diversified discursive global news sphere.

The final level in the hierarchy of influences, which is the *ideological level*, is one of the most difficult yet important levels that a foreign correspondent has to deal with. This is particularly evident when the foreign correspondent is reporting from one ideological perspective (the country being reported on) to another ideological perspective (the country or countries being reported to). The ideological level is 'concerned with how media symbolic content is connected with larger social interests, how meaning is constructed in the service of power' (Reese 2001: 183). Examples of ideological influences could be religious, political, or social positions, which hold influential power over the foreign correspondent and how they operate. For foreign correspondents, such influences are particularly evident since they shape the overall environment he or she is operating in. To add, any news discourse can either challenge or support a dominant ideological position, hence there is a power struggle at play here. Reese argues that the ideological level is influential in the construction of the media message as it is considered the 'cultural air' which 'provides the larger environment that journalists and their institutions occupy' (Reese 2001: 183).

The purpose of going through these influences, as modelled by Reese, is to outline the complexity of the differing levels through which foreign correspondents operate in when reporting within transcultural spheres. What it demonstrates is that there are many variables, factors, and powers at play when considering how a news discourse is to be shaped in global reporting. These influences also act as intersections where the culture of journalism that the foreign correspondent comes from can differ or clash with the local culture of journalism the foreign correspondent is reporting from. The need for foreign correspondents to tackle and address any cultural tensions that arise at these intersections is essential for producing journalism that assists in the formation of transcultural spheres. How the reporter manages to balance and relay differing dimensions throughout the hierarchy of influences is not easy, yet essential for future global reporting.

Throughout the FCST two-week period, participants were asked to produce four news stories. The first of these stories was always researched and pitched prior to departure to location and tended to focus on Australian relations to the country the participants were travelling to. The reason behind working on an 'Australian relations' story as an initial story, is to get participants to slowly familiarise themselves with the country they are travelling to through their own Australian frame. Examples of this have included Australian real estate companies operating in Dubai, Arab university students studying in Australian universities, and the difference in traditional Ayurvedic practices between India and Australia (see examples of this on: http://www.theforeigncorrespondent. org/our-reporting-1/). Although FCST participants were encouraged to find their story topics through their Australian cultural lens before travelling to the region they were meant to be reporting on, they were also asked to unpack the story while on location to discover other aspects of that story that could be translated through a transcultural lens. The aim of this process was to include a more accurate representation of reality in the stories produced through on-the-ground research and knowledge. The following quote from one participant on an FCST iteration to Jordan in 2016 illustrates this:

> I think what I'll take back to Australia from Jordan is probably an understanding of how important it is for stories to be nuanced. Umm, that you have to do the leg work, that you can't afford to make assumptions about

places I guess. I don't know, it's probably a huge generalisation to say that – oh no I don't think so - I guess the tour is here to challenge the assumptions that are made by Western media, and so getting here and talking to people and understanding that the stories here are just as complex as what happens in the West, has really made me realise that you can't take everything that is said about the Middle East for granted. You know you need to be - all of this needs to be taken with a grain of salt because these are just people living out human lives and I don't think that is a story that the Western media often tells. (Participant A)

Accordingly, through in-depth research and close interaction with the locals, the FCST participants were able to tell real stories about real people as best they could within a two-week time frame. The following quote from another participant from the 2016 FCST iteration to Jordan expands on this:

I think what I've learnt so far is that there are universals and there aren't. I think before coming to Jordan, I thought ... I don't know ... I thought the way I was thinking about the place was just completely wrong. When you get here and you talk to people you realise that really everybody's struggling with sort of human things, but then you understand as well that only being here for two weeks you can't ... you can't entirely understand a culture. You know the culture continues to sit just beyond our line of sight, I think. (Participant B)

The culture of journalism is also another factor to take into account when reporting within transcultural spheres. It is an aspect that reporters need to be open to. For example, one participant from the 2017 FCST Jordan iteration noted that the locals were extremely skilled in their story-telling techniques as part of their culture, and which was an aspect that local journalists utilised, as it also made it easy for reporters to relay their narratives. Since this form of storytelling amongst the sources was entrenched in the local culture, the participant noted that it was easier for her to tell their stories and report their perspectives than it was in Australia. This participant notes:

In addition, producing stories in Jordan was such a pleasure because it's clear there's a really strong tradition of storytelling. The people I interviewed, from Lina Khalifeh to Maria Haddad to Sister Adele to uni grads making video games, were so incredibly engaging. There were so many angles to each story, it was often difficult to pick one. (Participant G)

The aim of accurate representation of the local's realities, in essence therefore, is to counter mediated misrepresentations and fill in the missing discursive gaps. The privilege that foreign correspondents have is the ability to both physically and mentally access different cultural spheres, and then have the power to mediate between them. This is a rare privilege as the power to mediate these transcultural sphere is what distinguishes them from travellers, migrants and expatriates as noted before. One participant from the Jordan FCST iteration in 2016 during the US elections comments on this:

> Watching the US election in Amman, it became brutally clear how easy it is to live inside an echo chamber without even knowing it, the media we consume online is so tailored. The assumptions that we make aren't challenged until we visit somewhere that our media sources or Facebook network doesn't effectively reach. Visiting places like the Danish Refugee Council or the Italian Hospital or a Bedouin's tent are the kind of experiences that have not only helped to broaden my perspective but also make me think about how to effect real change through journalism. (Participant G)

Here we are not trying to prove what has already been evidenced and argued in the existing literature on the biases of news reporting and how news agendas are made to fit with institutional agendas (McChesney 2003), rather what we are arguing is the importance of foreign correspondents *actively* seeking to report on different discourses, representing other cultural news angles, and bridging gaps within transcultural spheres as discursive connections need to be made through news reporting. Essentially, therefore, what we argue is the need for foreign correspondents to prioritise establishing commonalities when mediating transcultural spheres, as more than often it is the differences that are emphasised in journalism practice. One FCST participant from a 2018 iteration points out the similarities and commonalities between various cultures which are not usually reported on:

> The ups-and-downs of the Jordanian people are not dissimilar to our own. As human beings, we all have our priorities, our insecurities and our fears. These are things borders and cultures can't change. (Participant I)

In addition to FSCT participants working with local journalists and interacting with the local people, part of the training activities was for the participants to spend time discussing the different journalism cultures that journalists from different countries operated in. Discussions with local journalists circulated around restrictions of freedom and how that impacted the processes and outcomes of their journalism. This gave the FCST participants enlightening perspectives on how foreign correspondents need to take these restrictions and different ways of doing journalism into account when reporting within transcultural spheres.

In this section, we have discussed the importance and necessity of foreign correspondents reporting within transcultural spheres, however in the following section we suggest taking this further by also reporting on positive angles through the notion of 'happy news'.

THE NOTION OF 'HAPPY NEWS'

As discussed thus far, news stories—especially on the global South—have tended to take on standardised formulas and set topics, rarely exploring different aspects, perspectives, or positive developments. Daya Kishan Thussu (2004) talks about this through what he labels as international journalism's 'poverty of news', where he states that there are 'absences' in global media content that result in a distorted view of parts of the developing world, as news about these regions are 'reduced to a simplistic version of often complex realities' (Thussu 2004: 55). He goes on to argue:

> With scant space to cover news from developing countries, these are often stereotyped into shorthand media clichés. While covering news of wars, disease, corruption and disasters in the South, international journalists are seldom encouraged by their editors to probe how the situation developed, how the event in question was related to its socio-economic and political environment, or to explore alternative viewpoints. As a result there is a steady underreporting of the cultural, economic, and political progress being made by developing countries. (Thussu 2004: 55)

Williams (2011) argues in his work that Western self-interest has traditionally been required for significant coverage of humanitarian crises, as foreign correspondents see it of interest to Western audiences. Yet future foreign correspondents need to approach their coverage without an agenda, with no self-interest, only an interest *in* others. He notes that 'the capacity of concerned individuals, organisations and bloggers to draw attention to international issues and attract public interest still depends on western gatekeepers, western news values, western interests and knowledge and western sources of information' (Williams 2011: 162). This interest has tended to focus on the *negative* framing of events.

Reporting negative news has been common practice in journalism, especially political reporting, since such journalism tends to want to take on the role of holding those in power accountable. Casey and Owen (2013) see journalism's role as countering that of government and politicians' self promotion. They state: 'Because governments promote their successes, it is natural that the role of accountability would focus on conveying negative news' (Casey and Owen 2013: 295). In global news, however, the focus on negative news has been dominant. Williams notes that '[r]ecent studies confirm the basic truth of Elliot and Golding's taxonomy – the coverage of the Third World is dominated by the "coups, wars, famines and disasters syndrome"' (Williams 2011: 156). Foreign correspondence has traditionally adopted a negative direction when reporting on various parts of the developing world, due to the notion that an event or issue is worth making the international news agenda only when something is wrong. Yet this has led to a decline in interest by audiences in international news, and they are left wondering 'what has the world come to'?

One of the issues, therefore, revolving around the decline of interest in foreign correspondence is what Susan Moeller (1999) labels as 'compassion fatigue'. In her work she questions why the media cover the world through trauma, conflict, and bad news in general. According to Moeller, compassion fatigue is the reason why international reporting is losing its ground amongst audiences. She argues that '[i]t is at the base of many of the complaints about the public's short attention span, the media's peripatetic journalism, the public's boredom with international news [...]' (Moeller 1999: 2). As a result, she notes, editors and journalists avoid covering issues and events that do not appeal to audiences. Hannerz (2012) confirms this, stating that audiences prefer to keep their distance from any negative news. He says:

> Since news of the world out there is so often bad news, news of conflicts and catastrophes, that world may seem to be above all a place to be wary of — one that on the basis of common sense the "man in the street" would want to have as little to do with as possible. You would prefer to keep your distance, and if people from out there knock on your door, you will want to send them away. (Hannerz 2012: 28–29)

The implications of this are severe, as it creates a transnational public sphere that lacks inclusiveness. Nancy Fraser (2007) has argued towards an inclusive transnational public sphere and suggests that a transnational public sphere be seen as a space where 'inclusiveness' is required in a 'postWestphalian' world and stresses the need to address not only 'who' is to emerge as participants but more importantly 'how' (Fraser 2007: 63), since these two questions are mutually inclusive. Moeller (1999) also relates to this in regards to compassion fatigue, stating that '[c]ompassion fatigue is not an unavoidable consequence of covering the news. It is, however, an unavoidable consequence of the way the news is now covered' (Moeller 1999: 2).

One way of addressing the *how* in promoting a transcultural sphere, as we argue in this volume, is through finding cultural connections that override the concept of the 'other' (Said 1978). News reports tend to focus on delivering stories that show other parts of the world, especially developing countries, as tragic, foreign, and miserable. News tends to frame the people of these nations as either victims or perpetrators, thus further increasing the gap between them and the global audience. This is indeed problematic, and as highlighted earlier, can lead to all sorts of social, political, or ideological repercussions that manifest in various aspects of everyday life. Recent research has shown that audiences are tired of tragic and depressing news, and as a result tend to avoid such news altogether. They selectively choose to veer away from stories that leave a 'bad taste in their mouth'. Antonis Kalogeropoulos labels this as 'avoidance audiences' and states that although the study he conducted looked at habits of audiences that did consume news, their research uncovered that audiences tried to avoid sad news. He explains that this can be seen as both 'avoidance stemming from the depressing nature of the content itself, and avoidance due to disapproval of the news media more broadly' (Kalogeropoulos 2017: 40).

Consequently, one recent trend in news that has come to tackle this issue is the idea of 'constructive journalism' or 'solutions journalism'. Online platforms such as *Constructive Journalism*, the *Solutions Journalism Network*, *Transformational Media*, and *Images & Voices of Hope (IVOH)*, have been on the rise to address just that. What constructive journalism aims to do is 'produce stories that give the audience a more comprehensive look around the issue at hand, focusing on solutions for problems rather than just the problems themselves' (Albeanu 2014). This 'comprehensive look' in news production means that audiences from around the world gain a clearer understanding of the issues being reported on from other countries, with the aim of understanding the reasons behind these events or why people from these places act the way they do. Ideally, finding 'solutions' as part of news reporting could lead to increased audience engagement and a sense of positivity.

Seán Dagan Wood, editor-in-chief of *Positive News* and co-founder of the *Constructive Journalism Project*, explains 'constructive' or 'solutions' journalism in a 2014 TEDx talk, saying that it is 'about bringing positive elements into conventional reporting, remaining dedicated to accuracy, truth, balance when necessary, and criticism, but reporting in a more engaging and empowering way' (quoted in McIntyre 2017: 3). There is a reason why journalism has tended to focus on negative and conflict-based news, which as Karen McIntyre (2017) believes is due to journalists—and humans in general—being connected to threats and drama, in addition to the media playing a watchdog role and thus intrinsically reporting on corruption (McIntyre 2017: 1), rather than positive developments in the world. McIntyre (2017) therefore explains the difference between solutions journalism and conventional reporting:

> Solutions journalism could be regarded as a niche form of journalism, but ultimately it need not be separate from mainstream journalism. Rather, more solutions-based ways of gathering and producing news could be incorporated into typical journalistic work. Proponents of solutions journalism say this practice embodies the values of traditional, objective journalism, as the reporters do not devise solutions on their own or seek to influence the story but rather choose story topics that showcase progress or growth and ask sources questions about potential solutions. (McIntyre 2017: 1)

Accordingly, rather than seeing constructive or solutions journalism as sitting outside traditional journalism practice, it can be incorporated in daily news reporting for that matter.

This is further emphasised through a study conducted by Cathrine Gyldensted (2011), Director of *Constructive Journalism in the Netherlands*, where 710 participants were asked to respond to their reactions to different versions of the same factual story. They were first asked to read a 'classic typical style' news report, that would contain what the Gyldensted describes as 'a high negative word ratio'; the second version was a 'victim narrative' which included an even higher negative ratio than the 'classic news report'. These two versions are typical of the format that journalists are taught to use and practice when reporting on a story, and also form the basis of reporting adopted by foreign correspondents. The participants, in different groups, were then introduced to four other versions of what Gyldensted says were structured as narratives that were 'based on key concepts in positive psychology': the first is the '3-to-1 positivity ratio', which combines both positive and negative framing with a higher positivity ratio; the second was structured on the 'peak/end rule', where positivity peaks towards the end of the story, similar to the framing of solutions journalism; the third is based on the 'meaningful narrative' which is overall a positive version of the story; and the final structure was a 'hero narrative', which opposite to the 'victim narrative' framing, and is based on a 'high positive word ratio' (Gyldensted 2011: 25).

This experiment sought to test whether audiences responded and engaged better with the more positive constructions of the story, than with the 'classic typical story' or the 'victim narrative'. The outcomes of this study indicated that, generally, participants had an increased positive affect to positive stories. Gyldensted articulates the results in more detail:

> Across conditions, participants significantly dropped in positive affect after reading the classical news story, with non-significant changes in affect after reading the second news story, regardless of condition [...] Reading the peak end narrative reduced negative affect the most in readers, followed by the 3-to-1 ratio and the hero narratives. Surprisingly, the meaning narrative, which was considered a positive version, increased negative affect in the reader. As expected, negative affect continued to increase in the negatively-valences victim narrative. (Gyldensted 2011: 26–27)

The reason why the meaning narrative, which is based on a positive framing, increased negative responses by participants is because they felt manipulated. Yet, Gyldensted notes that the participants 'did not highlight the negative manipulations in their feedback' from the 'classic typical story' or the victim story which contained a 'high negative word ratio', and which is due to them being normalised to such reporting, or as Gyldensted argues is due to 'desensitizing' as a result of constant exposure to such news styles (Gyldensted 2011: 31). Based on the above study, Gyldensted concludes that constructive journalism draws on positive psychology where journalists need to stop seeing the interviewees as victims, creating journalism that 'evokes awe and meaning' (Trenore 2014).

McIntyre argues that '[s]olutions journalism is one example of the type of journalism where the reporter takes a more active role' (McIntyre. 2017: 5). Although such positively-focused forms of journalism have evolved to actively challenge trends of negative framing in news, we suggest the notion of *happy news* can still include tragic aspects but does so by including positive aspects too when reporting other people and nations, as opposed to constantly framing them through a negative frame and portraying them as a distant 'other'. Through the notion of happy news, the reporter still takes on an active role however not by necessarily providing solutions, but rather by actively trying to bridge the gap and provide a holistic *factual* framing of the story or event at hand. In essence, therefore, a main difference here is that such news provides a positive framing of the country or the people being reported on, bridging cultural connections that allow the local and global to connect, without necessarily providing solutions.

Foreign correspondents have traditionally reported on conflict, death and tragedy. Audiences in turn have become disassociated and disengaged with such stories and images, enhancing the concept of the alien or 'other'. As part of the FCST project, reporters were clearly instructed and required to report on positive stories, meaning that they were required to show that people in the global South are not that dissimilar to those living in other parts of the world. Using the notion of 'happy news', FCST participants were asked to intentionally provide 'positive' stories on the locations they were visiting, especially in relation to the Middle East. By doing so, they would bring to Australian and global audiences a different account of a region of the world that is riddled with conflict, and often framed through a terrorism discourse. Hence students were asked to provide a counter-discourse to those found within mainstream Western media by simply reporting on stories through countering angles to those typically reported on.

Initially students were hesitant and uncomfortable with this brief, because they felt that they were expected to provide an 'embellished' account of reality. However, after spending time on location they understood that what they were asked to do was in fact to report on a more representative reality. One participant reflects on this in relation to an FCST iteration to Jordan in 2016:

I think before we left I was concerned by the stipulation that we were looking for positive stories. As students, a story's positivity had never before been a factor in determining its potential. Once we got over there, understanding just how negatively skewed most news coverage was, I understood much more what we were trying to do. We were undertaking journalism, but we were also trying to tip the scales back toward a point of balance. Working toward a point where, hopefully in the near future, less positive stories can be covered and not simply be lost in the flood of negativity already issuing from coverage of the Middle East. (Participant F)

The connections that the participants made with local sources made it possible for them to provide a more positive account of the events and issues they reported on. This also happens with international reporters, however they are often required not to get involved with their subjects for the sake of 'objectivity'. What this results in, however, is a limited understanding of the real concerns and fears that the locals have. The same participant had more to add to this:

Before travelling to Jordan, I had no way of contextualising the Middle East. That is not to suggest that two weeks in a single country has given me a comprehensive knowledge of the region. But it has provided me with counterbalances. When I read news about the Middle East, it's not just grainy images of soldiers firing artillery into the desert which spring to mind. Now there's also Shafi chipping away at a sculpture or Mu'ath organising a performance for the Al-Balad theatre. Whether or not the news concerns Jordan, it is still a reminder that despite the broad thrust of the 'Western' view of the Middle East, the region is full of people just doing people-y things. The uncomfortable silences I shared with Jordanians in many hotel elevators were no different, for instance, to those that Sydney's lifts have to offer. (Participant F)

Although the notion of 'happy news' might not sit well with many foreign correspondents and journalists in general, we argue that it is essential for bridging the gap between different cultures and peoples around the world, especially those that have become 'foreign' or 'alien', in the attempt to connect, familiarise, and understand the other. We illustrate this further in the following chapter through the discursive output of examples from the Foreign Correspondent Study Tour.

References

Albeanu, C. (2014, August 18). *Why Constructive Journalism Can Help Engage the Audience.* https://www.journalism.co.uk/news/why-constructive-journalism-can-help-engage-the-audience/s2/a557706/. Accessed 10 April 2018.

Bebawi, S. (2016). *Media Power and Global Television News: The Role of Al Jazeera English.* London: I.B. Tauris.

Casey, G. P., & Owen, A. L. (2013). Good News, Bad News, and Consumer Confidence. *Social Science Quarterly, 94*(1), 292–315.

Deuze, M. (2002). National News Cultures: A Comparison of Dutch, German, British, Australian and U.S. Journalists. *Journalism and Mass Communication Quarterly, 79*(1) (Spring), 134–149.

Fraser, N. (2007). Transnationalizing the Public Sphere: On the Legitimacy and Efficacy of Public Opinion in a Post Westphalian World. In S. Benhabib, I. Shapiro, & D. Petranovic (Eds.), *Identities, Affiliations, and Audiences* (pp. 45–66). Cambridge: Cambridge University Press.

Gyldensted, C. (2011). *Innovating News Journalism Through Positive Psychology.* University of Pennsylvania Scholarly Commons. https://repository.upenn.edu/cgi/viewcontent.cgi?article=1024&context=mapp_capstone. Accessed 16 April 2018.

Hanitzsch, T. (2007). Deconstructing Journalism Culture: Toward a Universal Theory. *Communication Theory, 4*(17), 367–385.

Hanitzsch, T. (2017, October). Professional Identity and Roles of Journalists. *Oxford Research Encyclopedia of Communication.* http://communication.oxfordre.com/view/10.1093/acrefore/9780190228613.001.0001/acrefore-9780190228613-e-95?print=pdf. Accessed 19 April 2018.

Hannerz, U. (2012). *Foreign News: Exploring the World of Foreign Correspondents.* Chicago: University of Chicago Press.

Hepp, A. (2015). *Transcultural Communication.* West Sussex: Wiley-Blackwell.

Kalogeropoulos, A. (2017). News Avoidance. *Reuters Institute Digital News Report 2017.* Reuters Institute for the Study of Journalism. https://reutersinstitute.politics.ox.ac.uk/sites/default/files/Digital%20News%20Report%202017%20web_0.pdf?utm_source=digitalnewsreport.org&utm_medium=referral. Accessed 16 May 2018.

McChesney, R. W. (2003). Corporate Media, Global Capitalism. In S. Cottle (Ed.), *Media Organization and Production* (pp. 27–39). London: Sage.

McIntyre, K. (2017). Solutions Journalism: The Effects of Including Solution Information in News Stories About Social Problems. *Journalism Practice,* 1–19. https://www.researchgate.net/publication/321811757_Solutions_Journalism_The_effects_of_including_solution_information_in_news_stories_about_social_problems.

Moeller, S. D. (1999). *Compassion Fatigue: How the Media Sell War, Famine, War and Death.* Oxon: Routledge.

O'Regan, J. P., & MacDonald, M. N. (2007). Cultural Relativism and the Discourse of Intercultural Communication: Aporias of Praxis in the Intercultural Public Sphere. *Language and Intercultural Communication, 7*(4), 267–278.

Reese, S. D. (2001). Understanding the Global Journalist: A Hierarchy-of-Influences Approach. *Journalism Studies, 2*(2), 173–187.

Said, E. (1978). *Orientalism.* London: Routledge & Kegan Paul.

Thussu, D. K. (2004). Media Plenty and the Poverty of News. In C. Paterson & A. Sreberny (Eds.), *International News in the Twenty-First Century* (pp. 47–61). Eastleigh: John Libby Publishing.

Trenore, M. J. (2014, September 2). How Constructive Journalism Can Improve the Way Media Makers Tell Stories. *IVOH.* http://ivoh.org/constructive-journalism/. Accessed 14 April 2018.

UNESCO Report by the International Commission for the Study of Communication Problems. (1980). *Communication and Society Today and Tomorrow, Many Voices One World: Towards a New More Just and More Efficient World Information and Communication Order.* London: Kogan Page; New York: Unipub; Paris: UNESCO.

UNESCO World Report. (2009). *Investing in Cultural Diversity and Intercultural Dialogue.* http://www.un.org/en/events/culturaldiversityday/pdf/Investing_in_cultural_diversity.pdf. Accessed 29 October 2017.

Williams, K. (2011). *International Journalism.* London: Sage.

Worlds of Journalism. (2012–2016). *Aggregated Tables for Key Variables.* http://www.worldsofjournalism.org/research/2012-2016-study/data-and-key-tables/. Accessed 19 May 2018.

Zelizer, B. (2005). The Culture of Journalism. In J. Curran & M. Gurevitch (Eds.), *Mass Media and Society* (4th ed., pp. 198–214). New York: Hodder Arnold.

CHAPTER 6

The Foreign Correspondent Study Tour

Abstract This chapter discusses the future of the foreign correspondent through the example of the *Foreign Correspondent Study Tour (FCST)* for Australian journalism university students. Funded by the Australian Department of Foreign Affairs and Trade (DFAT). the study tour is designed to offer students the opportunity to file news stories on the ground with real deadlines to a main Australian online media organisation, SBS Online, in order to emulate the 'foreign correspondent' experience. In turn, this study tour prepares them for future journalistic experiences within an international context by providing them with the tools to do journalism within another culture. There have been numerous observations that have come out of each of the iterations of the study tour, and this chapter will discuss them.

Keywords Foreign correspondent · Journalism education · Study tour · Cultures of journalism · International reporting · Local journalism · Global news

As outlined earlier in this book, the FCST is a project that was launched in 2015 and is designed to offer students the opportunity to file news stories on the ground with real deadlines to an Australian media organisation, in order to emulate a 'foreign correspondent' experience. Such

© The Author(s) 2019
S. Bebawi and M. Evans, *The Future Foreign Correspondent*,
https://doi.org/10.1007/978-3-030-01668-5_6

an experience can only be achieved by exposing students to an international study experience outside the classroom. In turn, this study tour provides them with the tools to do journalism within another culture; in addition to a practical application of the conceptual frameworks students have studied as part of their degree.

The project has been funded by the Australian government; namely the Australian Department of Foreign Affairs and Trade (DFAT) through the Council for Australian-Arab Relations (CAAR) and Australia-India Council (AIC) for postgraduate journalism students, and the New Colombo Plan (NCP) grants for undergraduate journalism students. The FCST has taken journalism students to Jordan, India and Philippines, and will continue to expand to include Tunisia, Thailand and Japan in coming years.

Students pitch their story ideas to the Special Broadcasting Service (SBS) Online, which is a public broadcaster. The main function of SBS through its charter 'is to provide multilingual and multicultural radio, television and digital media services that inform, educate and entertain all Australians and, in doing so, reflect Australia's multicultural society', and does so by culturally aiming to 'promote understanding and acceptance of the cultural, linguistic and ethnic diversity of the Australian people' (SBS Charter, 1 May 2018). This suits the aims of the FCST, which in line with the discussions from the previous chapter, seek to train and report future foreign correspondents on telling stories through transcultural spheres. These aims were also consistent with those of the above funders, which meant that all stakeholders in the project were aligned in wanting to bridge the mediated gaps between Australia and the rest of the non-English speaking world.

The main objective of the FCST, therefore, is to train future international reporters to understand journalism in different cultures, by conveying stories of societies, histories, ideologies, expectations, ethics and moralities that are unfamiliar to them, with the aim of addressing misconceptions of Australian and global media coverage of the non-Western world. In addition, it aims to normalise the 'other' thus striving to change or modify perceptions and understandings of various regions of the global South. Such taught and learnt practices would ideally create future foreign correspondents who will tell stories of different countries and people through a common intercultural lens. There have been numerous observations that have come out of each of the iterations of the FCST, and this chapter will conduct a mapping of the journey for some stories that were worked on during the project, referring back to challenges and arguments we have made in the volume thus far.

To illustrate this, three stories as case studies from the FCST are included here. These serve as examples and are, therefore, included to explain the process through which the news stories were developed during the FCST iterations, and accordingly are representative of the approach taken in training and producing stories for the FCST. These stories were published on SBS online (http://www.sbs.com.au/topics/source/foreign-correspondent-study-tour), namely *How Zumba is helping Syrian refugee women to heal, How meditation is helping the Middle East achieve Zen,* and *Life as a transgender woman in India.* To show the progression of these stories, each story will be mapped through three stages: (1) *navigation of the story,* (2) *communication of the story,* and (3) the *intercultural lens* of the story. The *navigation of the story* will provide the context by outlining the training and making of the story; the *communication of the story* will offer analysis of the components that highlight how the training behind the story translated into the published piece; and the third stage will discuss the significance of telling the story through an *intercultural lens* provided by the FCST.

Story 1: How Zumba Is Helping Syrian Refugee Women to Heal (SBS Online, 25 November 2016)

Navigation of the Story

The topic of Syrian refugees is at the forefront of stories reported on internationally when Jordan is in the news. Jordan has taken in the highest number of Syrian refugees since the start of the Syrian crisis, bringing the number to 657,000 registered Syrian refugees as of the start of 2017 (*Jordan Times,* 21 March 2017). On this basis, it was no wonder that participants wanted to work on Syrian refugee stories, emulating the reports that they had seen from their own media in Australia and around the world, such as BBC World, on this topic. The participants initially pitched stories that were based on visiting Syrian refugee camps, focusing on the hardships these refugees had to endure. Again they were reminded that the brief was to focus on 'positive' stories, which they found hard to frame given the severity of the topic. This story (https://www.sbs.com.au/topics/life/culture/article/2016/11/16/how-zumba-helping-syrian-refugee-women-heal), therefore, came as a result of one participant who wanted to visit a Syrian refugee camp in Irbid, North of Jordan, and talk to women. After further research upon arrival it was found that women Syrian refugees are in fact trying to address their unhappiness by doing Zumba classes at the International Rescue Committee. This story provided a good fit to the study tour brief in that it foregrounded a positive from within the refugee crisis. In other words, it did not portray the Syrian women as a focal point for pity, rather as a source of admiration in the way that they were dealing with their crisis.

There were two concerns that this female student had in preparation for the story: the first is that she had to travel to a refugee camp in a country that she did not know well and did not know the language; and the second is that the women did not want to be filmed or photographed making the possibility of producing an integrated story doubtful. The first problem was easily solvable as many foreign correspondents employ fixers and/or drivers who know the local area well and can assist the reporter, so that is how this issue was addressed. As for the second issue, the student had to navigate her way and slowly negotiate with the Syrian women upon arrival as to how to conduct the story. After careful understanding of the concerns of the Syrian women, the student suggested filming their feet only while they were in the Zumba class without showing their faces. This still made for good video as the movement, music and attitude of the class was captured in the video. As for the images, the student also suggested that she take a shot from the back of the Syrian women to make sure they were unidentifiable (see Fig. 6.1). Although these strategies are not uncommon in foreign reporting, the insistence to follow a story that gave another side to Syrian refugees and the willingness to navigate to understand the sensitivities and negotiate solutions to challenges that could have been an obstacle to the story are significant in this instance. As a result, the published story reflected a different discourse to what Western audiences were used to.

Fig. 6.1 Syrian refugees (*Credit* Yasmin Noone)

Communication of the Story

The story introduces the scene at the Zumba class describing how a *'female staff member donning a hijab is pumping a Zumba soundtrack [...] and also taking a personal moment to digest the Latino rhythms'*. Here the student is keen to provide an upbeat and positive start to the story. Other examples of this include:

> One by one, almost like a conga line, four staffers dance their way through the door of the room, their steps in sync to each hard salsa beat.
>
> It's a place where local women shed their burqas and hijabs to get their hair curled at the centre's beauty salon. Females of all ages gather to crochet, converse and learn English. And it's a place where Syrian refugees come to Zumba.

The story then moves on to explain the importance to why such *'activities help in healing and [help refugees to] recover from trauma activities'*.

The Syrian women themselves highlighted the impact of Zumba on them:

> When playing Zumba, everything in [my] body is moving. It is like it is positive energy. My health, my body, my soul and psychological life are now getting better and better.

However, it was always necessary for news pieces produced to also provide the 'serious' backdrop to the story. Although they were asked to provide counter-discourses to the gloomy portrayal of the Middle East in Western media, it was important to do this while giving an accurate account of the reality, hence there was a need to include the political issues behind the story:

> Amal says although Jordan is now her home, she "will never forget her country" or the many years she spent there.
> She hopes and prays to return to Syria one day and be reunited with the relatives, friends and neighbours she left behind.
> "We have suffered a lot. We have lost many things and I wish to get support with dignity.
> I just want my dignity, that's the main thing".

Intercultural Lens

Western media have been quick to portray the Syrian refugee crisis through various lenses; political, humanitarian crisis, environmental and even for political gain (Reuters 2015). Thus the innate training graduate journalism students have is to represent the same common themes. There is nothing wrong with these themes and these issues loom large as a result of the crisis. But by encouraging and empowering students to find a counter discourse to the crisis that resonates with their own cultural sensibilities (Stratton 2007), the reporter here tapped into a shared humanity that rises above normal representations. Zumba is a fitness program based around various dance styles that developed in the 1990s. Accredited to Columbian Alberto 'Beto' Perez, Zumba has traversed the globe, with estimates of 12–15 million people taking Zumba classes every week (A Short History of Zumba, 30 October 2017) in over 150 countries (Facts About Zumba, 31 October 2017). Zumba was 'designed to be low-impact, and to be an intense and efficient calo-rie-burning workout that is adaptable and suitable for all different ages, body types and levels of fitness' (A Short History of Zumba, 30 October 2017). While suitable for men, Zumba is heavily targeted to, and prac-ticed by, women. What the reporter discovers here then, is a cultural phenomenon completely familiar to her: women enjoying Zumba classes together for their mental and physical well-being. The concept is not one she needs to research or try to understand. Zumba is like breakfast, no explanation necessary. The point of difference is the location within a Syrian refugee camp inside Jordan. Take away that knowledge and this could be a Zumba class in any public school hall within a Muslim domi-nated suburb in Sydney. What the reporter latches onto is not the politi-cal, the hardship, the suffering, but the common humanity. She is all too aware of Zumba, it saturates her own life, why would it not therefore be part of these women's lives in Jordan. The FCST has taught her to look past the habitually presented discourses, and simply focus on the human-istic connection. Through embedding herself in this culture, and actively bringing her local cultural biases into view, she has crafted a story that speaks to groups of people all over the world. She has found the point of intercultural connection, and created a humanistic narrative that trans-forms the culture of international journalism.

STORY 2: HOW MEDITATION IS HELPING THE MIDDLE EAST ACHIEVE ZEN (SBS ONLINE, 24 NOVEMBER 2016)

Navigation of the Story

This story (https://www.sbs.com.au/topics/life/culture/article/2016/11/21/how-meditation-helping-middle-east-achieve-zen) talks about how people from different faiths in Jordan are gathering at the Dead Sea to meditate through Thai teachings. Again this story is not the average story that makes the daily news feed on the Arab world. At a time when ISIS still dominate the news, this story came to counter the extremist/terrorist portrayal of Arabs and Muslims in the region and rather demon-strate tolerance and humanity.

Despite the good intentions, this story was approached with some hesitation by the study tour leaders who understood some of the religious sensitivities involved, especially given it was within a dominant Muslim population that does not view Buddhism as a recognised religion (unlike Christianity or Judaism). Furthermore, Muslims are generally not in favour of the Dead Sea as a location due to its religious history in Islam, and therefore many believe it should not be visited. The student working on this story, however, was not aware of this religious context. In this instance, and unlike the previous story on refugees, the student became aware of the sensitivity of the topic during the editing phase, while working with the Local Consulting Producer who explained why the story had to do two things: (a) take into account the local audiences, and (b) provide an accurate portrayal of the social reality not from a Western lens but rather an intercultural lens. Examples of this will be now discussed.

Communication of the Story

The story starts with the description of a meditation scene at the Dead Sea—similar to how the previous refugee story begins with a description of the Zumba class:

> Under the light of the November supermoon sits a crowd of 350 Muslims, Christians and spiritualists looking out towards the Dead Sea.

The original lead to the story included the words '*Muslims, Christians and Buddhists*'. There was much discussion during the editing of the story about use of the word Buddhists at the start. Ultimately it was agreed that this should be changed to 'spiritualists' to have a softer impact on the local audiences. In this case, there was need for cultural sensitivity taking into account the local audience, while needing to remain true to the story. The word 'Buddhists' was included later on in the story, however the lead softly introduces the reader to the event and the different religious identities there. The story focused on examples of how this form of meditation works to unite people from different ideological backgrounds:

> "It was amazing how all these people gathered to do one thing: meditate," says teacher Nesreen Khashman, who helped guide the full moon session.

"We are creating a mediation movement now, with Muslims, Christians and Buddhists together," Khashman says. "[Because] what we are all searching for, regardless of our background, religious view or colour, is a better place where everyone can live in harmony".

The focus on harmony, on peace, is a counter discourse to the dominant tropes used to present the Middle East. Foreign correspondents (often embedded in military units) are tasked with reporting the military successes and defeats, the horrors of war and the human suffering that accompanies it. The Middle East is notoriously presented in terms of conflict and threat, but this story was dedicated to articulating peace and positivity:

So we have a slogan that we believe in: 'peace in, peace out'. If you cultivate the peace inside of you, you are able to do it for the whole world.

Further intensifying the meditation event was the fact that it took place at the Dead Sea, which borders Israel. But rather than focusing on this, or the religious contention of the Dead Sea, the story noted the factual:

So why is meditation taking off in the Middle East? Nassar believes meditation can help the diverse people of Jordan cope with current social pressures.

Jordan shares geographical borders with Syria, Iraq, Israel and Saudi Arabia. "We are living in a country that is located in between other Arab countries suffering from wars," says Nassar. "So because of that we have some issues more than other countries, like stress".

By portraying Islam as a peaceful religion, the piece was able to counter typical news stories about ISIS, for example, and the brutality their particular form of religion has brought:

One of the techniques mediation teaches you is to still your mind so that you can be mindful in praying or fasting. It's a technique that helps you to worship mindfully and it doesn't conflict with our religion.

Images also played an important role in providing a positive, peaceful portrayal of the meditation event. They were powerful tools to avoid any

Fig. 6.2   Jordanians meditating (*Credit* Yasmin Noone)

imagined misconceptions. For example, it was critical to portray veiled Muslim women happily and serenely participating in the event again counter to any discourses of resistance from them. Figure 6.2 shows two veiled Muslim women meditating with another man, breaking down various Western media depictions of spiritual adherence in the Middle East.

Intercultural Lens

In this example, the reporter was drawn to a story that resonated with her own experience, her own human lens. The concept of a large meditation event held during a supermoon at the Dead Sea was immediately arresting. The reporter was drawing on her understanding of the importance of the full moon in Buddhist spirituality (they view it as a sacred event) and the increasing popularity of meditation within first world Western countries. Traditional Buddhists observe a lunar calendar (as do Muslims thus creating a clear point of connection), and as such the moon is understood to be the centre of a Buddhists life. Indeed, '[i]n most Buddhist lineages, it is common to perform a special meditation ceremony on the full moon. Often, the ceremony includes a chant before sitting in silence and is followed by a candlelit procession' (Norrad 2017). The reporter captured the meditation chant used at the event and presented that as a sound file to accompany the story (How Meditation Is Helping the Middle East Achieve Zen, 30 October 2017). However, the story also captured an audience from another Western phenomena—mindfulness. Born from the same Buddhist teachings, mindfulness is a secularised, sanitised version of meditation currently sweeping Western countries and in particular, white-collar workplaces. Mindfulness programs are run to enhance employee 'well-being', as well as being taken up by individuals via mobile phone apps for personal happiness.

As noted above, what is significant in this example is that the reporter was unaware of the religious sensitivities such a gathering possessed. In bringing her own national Western/foreign axis to the story, and thus resonating with various groups internationally, what was missing was the local/foreign axis. It was vitally important that the story be sensitive to the various local nuances present. For instance, in developing the notion of meditation she was able to move past its current Western popularism to its religious historicity: *'Mediation may be a popular pastime in the West but here in the Middle East, it's an age-old practice'*. Here the importance of the cultural understanding and saturation provided by the FCST brought several aspects of the story to light, without distracting from the positivistic focus. Through working in the local context, with local content producers, and not simply filing from her own Western position, the reporter was able to craft the story to truly work interculturally. Despite the delicate and divisive religious, geographic and gendered concerns present, the story ultimately presented its point irrefutably: *'We are all human and we all deserve to have place where we can live in peace and happiness'*.

Story 3: Life as a Transgender Woman in India (SBS Online, 17 May 2018)

Navigation of the Story

When the reporter for this story first pitched the topic, there was some reluctance to include it in the FCST stories as it was addressing the sensitive topic of sexuality. Transgender in India have been treated as outcasts and as a result have had to resort to either street begging or prostitution. The reporter came across a community radio station in Bangalore that was run by transgenders for transgenders focusing on a transgender broadcaster called Priyanka, and hence found it to be an excellent opportunity to cover this story (https://www.sbs.com.au/topics/life/culture/article/2018/04/17/life-transgender-woman-india). Since the Karnataka cabinet had issued a legal policy in 2017 (*The India Express*, 27 October 2017) to recognise the rights of transgenders in India including the right to citizenship, which was previously denied, it was then decided that this would be a suitable story to address any misconceptions, especially that Australia had just undergone a referendum to recognise marriage equality in 2017. Hence this story not only held some resonance with Australian audiences, but also exposed them to commonalities with the Indian people who also constituted 7.4% of the Australian society born overseas, according to the Australian Bureau of Statistics (ABS) for 2016 (ABS 2016). It is also worth noting that this story was also a collaboration between an Australian FCST and an Indian journalism student, and therefore is not just an example of transcultural reporting in the output but also in the process.

Communication of the Story

The story tells the challenges of the transgender community in Bangalore and describes the hardships that they have had to undergo through the story of Priyanka who is a broadcaster for Radio Active, India's first transgender community radio station. The reporters conveyed this in their articles as follows:

> "We could only be sexual workers or beg because that was the only way we had some income. There was no other options instead of these. There were no other opportunities given to us in society. We had no choice but to do these things. We were forced into it," Priyanka said.
> We had no identity cards or shelter to stay and there was no voice for our community.

The story describes how Priyanka is now free to practice her rights and wear what she wants in the streets of Bangalore:

> Priyanka has become a voice at Radio Active for the transgender community.

"My program is called 'Yari Varu' and I can discuss topics including sexuality and non-acceptance by family members," she said.

"Earlier the transgender community was a lot smaller compared to now and most people didn't speak up about the difficulties. Now there are many NGOs and they can talk about all their problems."

One important aspect to this story is that it also gives a voice to the transgender community in India, which also aims to address the Indian diasporic community in Australia and beyond who might not be as supportive of the change of policy:

Although the policy protects the transgender community from discrimination and isolation, society still does not accept them.

"Our family members didn't accept us and usually kick us out of the house," Priyanka said.

"The one thing I want to tell the public is, you should give us an opportunity and only then we can tell you who we are and what we can do," she said.

Intercultural Lens

As noted in the previous two FCST stories on Jordan, this story on India is no different in that it seeks to portray commonalities at a humanistic level, which is that of basic human rights and civil equality. The FCST reporter sought to find a story that directly steered away from mainstream news discourses of poverty in India to that of a common theme of gender equality which was being discussed at the same time in a Western country such as Australia. Its importance also stems from the fact that it was a collaboration, with a byline by an Australian and Indian reporter, thus emphasising the importance of foreign correspondents working with local reporters to bring in both cultural perspectives. The Indian reporter, in this case, provided the historic plight of the transgender community, the cultural taboos associated with their existence, and their civil and legal rights that had recently been adopted. The Indian reporter would not have addressed this story had the Australian reporter not initiated the idea, ultimately leading to an example of how international reporting can lead to opening up in the discursive intercultural spheres.

Overall, the FCST has been designed as a tool for change. Every contemporary article will tell you that journalism is changing, and it is changing fast. So the obvious question arises about how we educate journalists for such a precarious future. One way, that also serves the increasingly important global context in which journalists work, is via teaching them how to navigate transcultural spheres and thus better represent local cultures within their work. They are writing for a transcultural, transnational audience, but need to do so grounded in the local knowledges and nuances that will create meaningful stories. As journalism continues to be outsourced, fragmented, freelanced and given individual autonomy, the onus is on educators to ensure future journalists are equipped with the cultural sensitivities that will empower and embolden society. The foreign correspondents of the future will be tools for social change, acting as conduits of local representation and intercultural understanding, particularly when it comes to regions of conflict and political/social/religious misconceptions.

Obviously some aspects of being a 'future' foreign correspondent will and must change, and yet some traditional skills remain fundamental and are yet to be further entrenched. One area that does need development is the need for more cultural understanding and representation of various voices within the global media sphere. Providing this will add to the 'culture of the journalist' and facilitate more equal, humanistic and engaged reporting to develop. The future of the FCST is not necessarily related to technological changes, rather it needs to focus on addressing misconceptions of global reporting in relation to representation of actual cultural realities. By doing so it will foster more cultural understanding for transcultural awareness especially surrounding political, social, and religious issues around the world.

Berglez (2008) has questioned whether our disposition towards domestic outlooks, our socioculturally ingrained mode of interpreting the world, is simply too strong and dominant? The FCST offers proof that this is not the case. With boundaries and space to explore the local, even transcultural reporting can represent that which speaks to the local and the international through a humanistic lens. The impetus is on striving for understanding, on the point of connection. It is knowing that every societal issue has unique nuances that need to be understood and appreciated. It is not merely about knowing, it is about knowing what you don't know. As one FCST participant prophetically noted: 'You know the culture continues to sit just beyond our line of sight' (Participant B).

REFERENCES

A Short History of Zumba. http://womensfitnessclubs.com/blog/2012/07/17/a-short-history-of-zumba/. Accessed 30 October 2017.

Australian Bureau of Statistics (ABS). (2016). *Cultural Diversity in Australia Census.* http://www.abs.gov.au/ausstats/abs@.nsf/Lookup/by%20Subject/2071.0~2016~Main%20Features~Cultural%20Diversity%20Article~60. Accessed 26 May 2018.

Berglez, P. (2008). What Is Global Journalism? *Journalism Studies, 9*(6), 845–858.

Facts About Zumba. https://www.thefactsite.com/2013/06/zumba-fitness-facts.html. Accessed 31 October 2017.

How Meditation is Helping the Middle East Achieve Zen. (2016, November 24). http://www.sbs.com.au/topics/life/culture/article/2016/11/21/how-meditation-helping-middle-east-achieve-zen. 30 October 2017.

Jordan Times. (2017, March 21). Jordan Hosts 657,000 Registered Syrian Refugees. http://www.jordantimes.com/news/local/jordan-hosts-657000-registered-syrian-refugees. Accessed 20 October 2017.

Norrad, S. (2017, March 10). *How to Celebrate the Full Moon Like a Buddhist.* https://www.elephantjournal.com/2017/03/how-to-celebrate-the-full-moon-like a-buddhist/. Accessed 31 October 2017.

Reuters. (2015, December 19). *Bigotry, Panic Reflected in Media Coverage of Migrants and Refugees.* https://www.reuters.com/article/us-refugees-media/bigotry-panic-reflected-in-media-coverage-of-migrants-and-refugees-idUSKBN0U129620151218. Accessed 31 October 2017.

SBS. (2016, November 24). *How Meditation Is Helping the Middle East Achieve Zen.* http://www.sbs.com.au/topics/life/culture/article/2016/11/21/how-meditation-helping-middle-east-achieve-zen. Accessed 22 October 2017.

SBS. (2016, November 25). *How Zumba Is Helping Syrian Refugee Women to Heal.* http://www.sbs.com.au/topics/life/culture/article/2016/11/16/how-zumba-helping-syrian-refugee-women-he. Accessed 22 October 2017.

SBS Charter. https://www.sbs.com.au/aboutus/corporate/index/id/25/h/SBS-Charter. Accessed 1 May 2018.

Stratton, J. (2007). *Australian Rock: Essays on Popular Music.* Perth: Network Books.

The India Express. (2017, October 27). Transgender Policy Cleared by Karnataka Cabinet. http://indianexpress.com/article/india/transgender-policy-cleared-by-karnataka-cabinet-4909196/. 27 May 2018.

CHAPTER 7

Conclusion: Future Possibilities

Abstract This final chapter will summarise the main points that *The Future Foreign Correspondent* book makes and discusses them in light of future challenges and opportunities that a digital news landscape offers. It will outline how some aspects of being a 'future' foreign correspondent will and must change, and yet how some traditional skills remain important but are still to be further entrenched, such as the need for more cultural understanding within the global media sphere.

Keywords Foreign correspondent · Future of journalism · Digital news

Underlining this volume has been the basic question of whether a foreign correspondent is still required in today's media environment. Technological advances, along with financial restrictions facing many media organisations, have seemingly made the foreign correspondent more precarious. We have sought to demonstrate here some of the ideological and practical situations under which we see foreign correspondents not only as important, but vital to the milieu of future journalism. That is not to say that things can necessarily continue as is, but that a greater appreciation of the transcultural sphere is going to be crucial in the future. We have debated whether the long-held tenets of journalism, its status as objective commentator, still hold? Of course, there has always been biased or partisan journalism, even propaganda, but now some would have us believe the line is blurred across all forms. 'Fake news', a concept that has really existed ever since we started reporting anything to each other at all, can now be bandied about for political gain, to avoid scandal, or to obfuscate more generally.

Jeff Jarvis reminds us that '[t]he idea of outcomes-orientated journalism requires that we respect the public and what it knows and needs and wants to know' (2014: 22). Future foreign correspondent journalism is exactly about that. Respecting the public means understanding them and what they want to be informed about. So often modern journalism presents information to the public assuming that's what they want, or worse, that is who they are. The future foreign correspondent has an opportunity to be positioned differently. As Jarvis continues, 'journalism is helping citizens and communities meet their needs and accomplish their goals. Journalism is a tool to improve society' (2014: 49). Foreign correspondents are part of that mission, with even greater recourse to connect citizens, communities and nations.

Finding Our Depth

Throughout this volume we have touched on the issue of completeness, thoroughness, and basically depth of reporting. Steve Sammartino, a futurist and not a journalist—or even a commentator on journalism—has this to say: 'Fast news is like fast food. It has very little intellectual value. Slow news is what we ought to focus on' (Sammartino 2017: 171). This is an idea that is easy to skip over—but should we? Sure it reads like a soundbite designed to provoke rather than inform, but is there something behind the catchphrase we as journalism scholars need to heed. 'Fast news' surrounds us, and an increasingly compressed industry founded on it. The faster the better; immediacy over accuracy. But there is another way to consider journalism in this digital age. This approach concerns depth, it is developed slowly through detailed observation and cultural synthesis. For the foreign correspondent the fast is tempting, it is promotional and presumably career advancing, but shallow over all. What we have argued in this volume is that depth and, to some degree, assimilation is important. At the very least, detailed cultural sensitivity based on local understanding is a must. One FCST participant to India reflects:

I was in a country I'd never been to before, not able to speak the language, with people that weren't my friends or family (yet). Sitting on kitchen floors with women I'd met just hours earlier talking pads and menstrual cups and contraception, watching young girls in a village take photos of one another with my camera, having dinner at Saswati's home and listening to her and her mother sing, visiting the neonatal unit in a women's hospital, dancing the night away in an African club... I felt the fear and anxiety and I did things anyway. I asked strangers questions. I spoke to people on the streets, in pubs, in shopping centres and restaurants. In clubs, at food festivals, in villages and in hospitals. I learnt to be less precious [...] That who I am as a person and who I am as a journalist can, and sometimes must, be different. (Participant K)

Here we see Participant K embracing, living the cultural synthesis and developing a greater cultural sensitivity as a result. Not always comfortable or easy, but Participant K lays out the raw humanism of their experience and the effects of that on their journalism and their sense of self.

To that end the fast food analogy might work—it tastes good and satisfies us briefly but ultimately has little nutritional value. We need to train people who are providing the fullest smorgasbord possible, respecting the public (Jarvis 2014) and making a difference to the flow of information. Crawford et al. (2015) speak of depth through countering the forces that produce the shallow, they write:

Everything we are learning points in the same direction: the key to digital success in the new world is not simply to better understand the Facebook algorithm. The key is to go where the platform providers don't want to: deeper 'inside the packet', into the stories themselves. Here, in the narrative atoms being shuffled around networks, you find what is most valuable to people [...] The story structures and topics that resonate most strongly now are the ones that will be around long after the last Facebook profile has been uploaded. (Crawford et al. 2015: 285)

That has been a key argument of this volume, that journalists—and specifically foreign correspondents—need to go deeper into the stories themselves. For us, the 'packet' is the multi-faceted cultural milieu that is fed into the story. For us, it is the multiple voices that bring their perspectives to the story. For us (and Zelizer 2005), it is the many cultures the journalists themselves bring to the story. We worry about the algorithm, about clickability, instead of supporting those whose stories are being told. As Jarvis points out: 'In the future, journalists much ask: How do we encourage and support flows of information?' (2014: 61).

The Foreign Correspondent Study Tour as Prototype

The inspiration for this volume, the Foreign Correspondent Study Tour (FCST), has provided a glimpse of what future foreign correspondents might look like. As we have shown in Chapter Six, students today are surrounded by media yet do not necessarily understand places, peoples, and cultures different to their own. At least from our Western perspective, students were shocked and surprised by other cultures, and by their flimsy understanding of them. Through the FCST they discovered their own learning processes in relation to the 'other'. They also matured through the process of the FCST, and came to understand their own cultures of journalism. On top of that, they understood *why* they were the way they were, and *how* they had been constructed. One participant states in relation to this:

> This trip has been beneficial is so many ways. Not only have I learned things which benefit me as a journalist, but I've also learned things which benefit me as a person. The ups-and-downs of the Jordanian people are not dissimilar to our own. As human beings, we all have our priorities, our insecurities and our fears. These are things borders and cultures can't change. Caught between regional conflict and economic turmoil, it's still inspiring how optimistic the Jordanian people are. They know their livelihoods could change at any moment and yet they still greet you with a smile and ask you how your day is going. The people I've met, interviewed and written about on this trip are amazing. Each one has considerable odds stacked against them; whether that be Mohammed Zakaria with his publicly funded skate park, Rula Quawas teaching feminism at a conservative school or Ahmad Satti struggling to make it in a society hesitant to embrace hip-hop. These are just three people. Jordan has a population of more than six million people- that's six million stories just waiting to be told. (Participant Q)

We have also seen the power of bringing new images and stories to the fore. Of being willing to present alternate narratives about people and places that challenge the dominant discourse. As Williams (2011) notes: 'Clutching on to clichés and well trodden stereotypes is often how journalists attempt to make sense of situations and societies with which they and their audiences are unfamiliar' (Williams 2011: 153). The future foreign correspondent need not be bound by these stereotypes, need not settle for the lowest common denominator. Partly this is a problem of some journalism education. Students are trained in local journalism—which, if done at the expense of other forms is detrimental enough—where they seek out one side of the story and then the other. But in foreign settings that approach might not work. Sources may choose not to tell you the truth for a legion of reasons, reasons that can only be understood through an intercultural lens. There are rich stories to be told, and complicated lives behind them. There may well be a tension to be held, a tension that defies easy solutions and that certainly rejects clichés.

The FCST has allowed us to think beyond the dominant tropes of international news. It has allowed us to imagine what it might be. As Williams rightly points out, '[i]nternational news is characterized by less diversity of opinion and viewpoint' (2011: 154). This is what the FCST is trying to counter. We cannot add value to the flow of information if we narrow the range of opinions. One participant from the India FCST states:

> Throughout this experience, I learnt that journalists need to be confident and learn how to eliminate personal views from any story they are assigned to. No matter your view on a particular issue or story, the job of a journalist is to present the story of the individual or incident, excluding all personal judgements and opinions. Whilst researching and writing my story on the transgender community in Bangalore, I had to be mindful about the way I approached this topic, as I was unsure about how sensitive the topic was. It was a challenging story, as I was unsure what interview questions would be suitable to ask and how much the sources would potentially reveal or like to talk about. However, I learnt that in order to deal with such stories, you need to be direct and honest about your approach with everyone involved in the story. (Participant L)

Diversity is vital to future foreign correspondence, even if it means training new journalists who are conversant in intercultural dialogues that will benefit all concerned. In order to do that we need to provide community and relationships to students as they are studying. We need to be able to connect them with relevant groups of people to both diversify their thinking, but also teach them to connect with others and themselves in the future. As Jarvis reminds us, '[i]t is difficult to teach students interactive journalism when they don't have a community with whom to interact' (2014: 212). It will be impossible for future foreign correspondents to relay the depth of the story if they are unable to connect into the relevant community. Again, journalism has become about relationship (Jarvis 2014). Some journalism educators advocate (and utilise) a 'teaching hospital' model for journalism schools. We propose the FCST is merely one intense version of such a construct. Students are working on real stories but answerable to real people, real communities. And we want their new vision to break down the trusted, accepted approaches to foreign correspondence. Students today 'see the world in new ways' (Jarvis 2014: 214) and so should have opportunity to practice their craft in new ways as well. As educators our job is to open up the possibilities.

A Valuable Future

Sammartino argues that to understand what will become valuable in our future society we merely need to be aware of what is becoming scarce now. He provides the following list of elements in our contemporary lives that are in increasingly short supply:

> People's attention, our privacy, physical space, access to nature, face-to-face contact, personal service, curation of valuable content, interface design, service design, craftwork, filtering of data, making sense of data points, human performance, art, creativity. (Sammartino 2017: 116)

So much of this list intersects with the foreign correspondent. To this end, the future value that they will add to the flow of information can indeed be rich. They need to be about people, relationships, the face-to-face. They will be invaluable curators of content, collecting, filtering and making connections that tell real stories that captivate people's attention. They will perform their knowledge, but more importantly they will live their questions. This is because '[q]uestion makers will be seen, properly, as the engines that generate the new fields, new industries, new brands, new possibilities, new continents that our restless species can explore. Questioning is simply more powerful than answering' (Kelly 2016: 289). The future foreign correspondent will question and probe through their intercultural lens, from a place of genuine interest and empathy. They will question what the right communities are for the questions to be answered. They will interrogate the flows of information that wiz past them. They will question the dominance of the negative when positive stories are there to be told. They will question their own biases towards the subjects they seek out. 'A good question is what humans are for' (Kelly 2016: 289)—this is not a job for robots.

REFERENCES

Crawford, H., Hunter, A., & Filipovic, D. (2015). *All Your Friends Like This: How Social Networks Took Over News*. Sydney: HarperCollins.

Jarvis, J. (2014). *Geeks Bearing Gifts: Imagining New Futures For News*. New York: CUNY Journalism Press.

Kelly, K. (2016). *The Inevitable: Understanding the 12 Technological Forces That Will Shape Our Future*. New York: Penguin Books.

Sammartino, S. (2017). *The Lessons School Forgot*. Milton, QLD: Wiley.

Williams, K. (2011). *International Journalism*. London: Sage.

Zelizer, B. (2005). The Culture of Journalism. In J. Curran & M. Gurevitch (Eds.), *Mass Media and Society* (4th ed., pp. 198–214). New York: Hodder Arnold.

REFERENCES

A Short History of Zumba. http://womensfitnessclubs.com/blog/2012/07/17/a-short-history-of-zumba/. Accessed 30 October 2017.

Albeanu, C. (2014, August 18). *Why Constructive Journalism Can Help Engage the Audience*. https://www.journalism.co.uk/news/why-constructive-journalism-can-help-engage-the-audience/s2/a557706/. Accessed 10 April 2018.

Allen, B. (2013, January 23). A Brave Young Journalist in Jordan. *Journalists for Human Rights*. http://www.jhr.ca/blog/2013/01/a-brave-young-journalists-in-jordan/. Accessed 5 December 2014.

Almadhoun, S. (2010). Status of Freedom of Information Legislation.

Amanpour, C. (2012). *Objectivity in War*. https://www.youtube.com/watch?v=tqwYyAzux6M. Accessed 14 May 2018.

Anderson, C. W., Bell, E., & Shirky, C. (2012). *Post-industrial Journalism: Adapting to the Present*. New York: Tow Centre for Digital Journalism, Columbia University.

Archetti, C. (2012). Which Future for Foreign Correspondence?: London Foreign Correspondents in the Age of Global Media. *Journalism Studies, 13*(5–6), 847–856.

Aucoin, J. (2006). *The Evolution of American Investigative Journalism*. Columbia: University of Missouri Press.

Australian Bureau of Statistics (ABS). (2016). *Cultural Diversity in Australia Census*. http://www.abs.gov.au/ausstats/abs@.nsf/Lookup/by%20Subject/2071.0~2016~Main%20Features~Cultural%20Diversity%20Article~60. Accessed 26 May 2018.

Bebawi, S. (2016a). *Media Power and Global Television News: The Role of Al Jazeera English*. London: I.B. Tauris.

© The Editor(s) (if applicable) and The Author(s) 2019
S. Bebawi and M. Evans, *The Future Foreign Correspondent*,
https://doi.org/10.1007/978-3-030-01668-5

Bebawi, S. (2016b). *Investigative Journalism in the Arab World: Issues and Challenges.* London: Palgrave.

Berglez, P. (2008). What Is Global Journalism? *Journalism Studies, 9*(6), 845–858.

Berret, C., & Phillips, C. (2016). *Teaching Data and Computational Journalism.* New York: Columbia Journalism School.

Borovik, A. (2001). *The Hidden Way: A Russian Journalist's Account of the Soviet War in Afghanistan.* New York: Grove Press.

Bossio, D., & Bebawi, S. (2012). Reaping and Sowing the News from an Arab Spring: The Politicised Interaction Between Traditional and Alternative Journalistic Practitioners. *Global Media Journal: Australian Edition, 2*(6). https://www.hca.westernsydney.edu.au/gmjau/archive/v6_2012_2/pdf/bossio_bebawi_RA_V6-2_2012_GMJAU.pdf. Accessed 20 January 2017.

Boyd-Barrett, O. (2002). Theory in Media Research. In C. Newbold, O. Boyd-Barrett, & H. Van Den Bulck (Eds.), *The Media Book* (pp. 1–54). London: Arnold.

Bunce, M. (2015). Africa in the Click Stream: Audience Metrics and Foreign Correspondents in Africa. *African Journalism Studies, 36*(4), 12–29.

Campbell, C. (2017). *World Press Trends 2017.* Frankfurt: WAN-IFRA.

Casey, G. P., & Owen, A. L. (2013). Good News, Bad News, and Consumer Confidence. *Social Science Quarterly, 94*(1), 292–315.

Cooke, R. (2008, April 14). Man of War. *The Guardian.* https://www.theguardian.com/media/2008/apr/13/middleeastthemedia.lebanon. Accessed 16 May 2018.

Cottle, S. (2009). Journalism Studies: Coming of (Global) Age? *Journalism, 10*(3), 309–311.

Couldry, N. (2000). *The Place of Media Power: Pilgrims and Witnesses of the Media Age.* London: Routledge.

Couldry, N. (2003). Beyond the Hall of Mirrors? Some Theoretical Reflections on the Global Contestation of Media Power. In N. Couldry & J. Curran (Eds.), *Contesting Media Power: Alternative Media in a Networked World* (pp. 39–54). Oxford: Rowman & Littlefield.

Couldry, N., & Curran, J. (2003). The Paradox of Media Power. In N. Couldry & J. Curran (Eds.), *Contesting Media Power: Alternative Media in a Networked World* (pp. 3–15). Oxford: Rowman & Littlefield.

Couldry, N., & Hepp, A. (2017). *The Mediated Construction of Reality.* Cambridge: Polity Press.

Crawford, H., Hunter, A., & Filipovic, D. (2015). *All Your Friends Like This: How Social Networks Took Over News.* Sydney: HarperCollins.

Dahlby, T. (2014). *Into the Field: A Foreign Correspondent's Notebook.* Austin: University of Texas Press.

De Burgh, H. (2005). Introduction. In H. de Burgh (Ed.), *Making Journalists: Diverse Models, Global Issues* (pp. 1–21). Florence: Taylor & Francis.

Deuze, M. (2002). National News Cultures: A Comparison of Dutch, German, British, Australian and U.S. Journalists. *Journalism and Mass Communication Quarterly, 79*(1) (Spring), 134–149.

Deuze, M. (2006). Global Journalism Education. *Journalism Studies, 7*(1), 19–34.

Facts About Zumba. https://www.thefactsite.com/2013/06/zumba-fitness-facts.html. Accessed 31 October 2017.

Filkins, D. (2009). *The Forever War*. New York: Vintage.

Fraser, N. (2007). Transnationalizing the Public Sphere: On the Legitimacy and Efficacy of Public Opinion in a Post Westphalian World. In S. Benhabib, I. Shapiro, & D. Petranovic (Eds.), *Identities, Affiliations, and Audiences* (pp. 45–66). Cambridge: Cambridge University Press.

Gellhorn, M. (1994). *The Face of War*. New York: Atlantic Monthly Press.

Gentzkow, M., & Shapiro, J. M. (2010). What Drives Media Slant? Evidence from U.S. Daily Newspapers. *Econometrica, 78*(1), 35–71.

Greenway, H. D. S. (2014). *Foreign Correspondent: A Memoir*. New York: Simon & Schuster.

Gyldensted, C. (2011). *Innovating News Journalism Through Positive Psychology*. University of Pennsylvania Scholarly Commons. https://repository.upenn.edu/cgi/viewcontent.cgi?article=1024&context=mapp_capstone. Accessed 16 April 2018.

Hachten, W. A., & Scotton, J. F. (2007). *The World News Prism: Global Information in a Satellite Age*. Oxford: Blackwell.

Hafez, K. (2007). *The Myth of Media Globalization*. Cambridge: Polity Press.

Hamilton, J. M. (2009). *Journalism's Roving Eye: A History of American Foreign Reporting*. Baton Rouge: Louisiana State University Press.

Hamilton, J. M., & Jenner, E. (2004). Redefining Foreign Correspondence. *Journalism, 5*(3), 301–321.

Hamilton, J. M., & Perlmutter, D. D. (2007). *From Pigeons to News Portals: Foreign Reporting and the Challenge of New Technology* (M. H. John & D. D. Perlmutter, Eds.). Baton Rouge: Louisiana State University Press.

Hannerz, U. (2012). *Foreign News: Exploring the World of Foreign Correspondents*. Chicago: University of Chicago Press.

Hanitzsch, T. (2007). Deconstructing Journalism Culture: Toward a Universal Theory. *Communication Theory, 4*(17), 367–385.

Hanitzsch, T. (2017, October). Professional Identity and Roles of Journalists. In *Oxford Research Encyclopedia of Communication*. http://communication.oxfordre.com/view/10.1093/acrefore/9780190228613.001.0001/acrefore-9780190228613-e-95?print=pdf. Accessed 19 April 2018.

Hepp, A. (2015). *Transcultural Communication*. West Sussex: Wiley Blackwell.

Herbert, J. (2013). *Practising Global Journalism: Exploring Reporting Issues Worldwide*. New York: Focal Press.

How Meditation Is Helping the Middle East Achieve Zen. (2016, November 24). http://www.sbs.com.au/topics/life/culture/article/2016/11/21/how-meditation-helping-middle-east-achieve-zen. Accessed 30 October 2017.

Howie, S. (2016, December 12). Interview with Saba Bebawi, Vice President for Professional Development at GMA Network. Manila, Philippines.

Jarvis, J. (2014). *Geeks Bearing Gifts: Imagining New Futures for News.* New York: CUNY Journalism Press.

Johnson, T. (2015, March). Desert Storm: The First War Televised Live Around the World (and Around the Clock). *Atlanta Magazine.* http://www.atlantamagazine.com/90s/desert-storm-the-first-war-televised-live-around-the-world-and-around-the-clock/. Accessed 19 April 2018.

Jordan Times. (2017, March 21). Jordan Hosts 657,000 Registered Syrian Refugees. http://www.jordantimes.com/news/local/jordan-hosts-657000-registered-syrian-refugees. Accessed 20 October 2017.

Kalogeropoulos, A. (2017). News Avoidance. *Reuters Institute Digital News Report 2017.* Reuters Institute for the Study of Journalism. https://reutersinstitute.politics.ox.ac.uk/sites/default/files/Digital%20News%20Report%202017%20web_0.pdf?utm_source=digitalnewsreport.org&utm_medium=referral. Accessed 16 May 2018.

Kelly, K. (2016). *The Inevitable: Understanding the 12 Technological Forces That Will Shape Our Future.* New York: Penguin Books.

Lacey, M. (2017, June 14). What's the Difference Between a Reporter and a Correspondent? *The New York Times.* https://www.nytimes.com/2017/06/14/insider/whats-the-difference-between-a-reporter-and-a-correspondent.html. Accessed 2 June 2018.

Lecompte, C. (2015, September 2). From Nieman Reports: From Earnings Reports to Baseball Recaps, Automation and Algorithms are Becoming a Bigger Part of the News. *Nieman Lab.* http://www.niemanlab.org/2015/09/from-nieman-reports-from-earnings-reports-to-baseball-recaps-automation-and-algorithms-are-becoming-a-bigger-part-of-the-news/. Accessed 22 May 2018.

Lim, S. (2017, September 27). Legacy Media Organisations Are Paying the Price for Slow Pivot to Digital Disruption, Experts Say. *The Drum.* http://www.thedrum.com/news/2017/09/27/legacy-media-organisations-are-paying-the-price-slow-pivot-digital-disruption. Accessed 30 June 2018.

Lindell, J., & Karlsson, M. (2016). Cosmopolitan Journalists? *Journalism Studies, 17*(7), 860–870.

Macnamara, J. (2014). *Journalism & PR: Unpacking Spin Stereotypes and Media Myths.* New York: Peter Lang.

Matthews, J. (2013). Journalists and Their Sources: The Twin Challenges of Diversity and Verification. In K. Fowler-Watt & S. Allan (Eds.), *Journalism: New Challenges* (pp. 242–258). Bournemouth: Centre for Journalism & Communication Research, Bournemouth University.

McChesney, R. W. (2003). Corporate Media, Global Capitalism. In S. Cottle (Ed.), *Media Organization and Production* (pp. 27–39). London: Sage.

McIntyre, K. (2017). Solutions Journalism: The Effects of Including Solution Information in News Stories About Social Problems. *Journalism Practice*, 1–19. https://www.researchgate.net/publication/321811757_Solutions_ Journalism_The_effects_of_including_solution_information_in_news_stories_ about_social_problems.

McNair, B. (2005). Introduction. In H. de Burgh (Ed.), *Making Journalists: Diverse Models, Global Issues* (pp. 25–43). Florence: Taylor & Francis.

McNair, B. (2017). *Fake News: Falsehood, Fabrication and Fantasy in Journalism.* New York: Routledge.

Miller, A. (1953). *The Crucible.* New York: Viking Press.

Moeller, S. D. (1999). *Compassion Fatigue: How the Media Sell War, Famine, War and Death.* Oxon: Routledge.

Mungham, G. (1987). Israel: Fog Over Lebanon. In D. Mercer, G. Mungham, & K. Williams (Eds.), *The Fog of War: The Media on the Battlefield* (pp. 261–290). London: Heinemann.

Murdock, G., & Golding, P. (2005). Culture, Communications and Political Economy. In J. Curran & M. Gurevitch (Eds.), *Mass Media and Society* (4th ed., pp. 60–83). London: Hodder Arnold.

Murrell, C. (2015). *Foreign Correspondents and International Newsgathering: The Role of Fixers.* New York: Routledge.

Newman, N., Fletcher, R., Kalogeropoulos, A., Levy, D. A. L., and Nielsen, R. K. (2017). *Reuters Institute Digital News Report 2017.* Reuters Institute for the Study of Journalism. https://reutersinstitute.politics.ox.ac.uk/sites/default/ files/Digital%20News%20Report%202017%20web_0.pdf?utm_source=digital-newsreport.org&utm_medium=referral. Accessed 16 May 2018.

Nickerson, R. S. (1998). Confirmation Bias: A Ubiquitous Phenomenon in Many Guises. *Review of General Psychology, 2*(2), 175–220.

Nielson, R. K., & Sambrook, R. (2016). *What Is Happening to Television News?* Digital News Project 2016. Reuters Institute for the Study of Journalism. http://reutersinstitute.politics.ox.ac.uk/sites/default/files/2017-06/What%20 is%20Happening%20to%20Television%20News.pdf. Accessed 15 May 2018.

Norrad, S. (2017, March 10). *How to Celebrate the Full Moon like a Buddhist.* https://www.elephantjournal.com/2017/03/how-to-celebrate-the-full-moon-like-a-buddhist/. Accessed 31 October 2017.

O'Regan, J. P., & MacDonald, M. N. (2007). Cultural Relativism and the Discourse of Intercultural Communication: Aporias of Praxis in the Intercultural Public Sphere. *Language and Intercultural Communication, 7*(4), 267–278.

Penny, L. (2017, January 20–26). Escape from Reality: Fake News Sells Because People Want It to Be True. *New Statesman*, pp. 18–19.

Rai, M., & Cottle, S. (2007). Global Mediations: On the Changing Ecology of Satellite Television News. *Global Media and Communication, 3*(51), 51–78.

Reese, S. D. (2001). Understanding the Global Journalist: A Hierarchy-of-Influences Approach. *Journalism Studies, 2*(2), 173–187.

Reuters. (2015, December 19). *Bigotry, Panic Reflected in Media Coverage of Migrants and Refugees.* https://www.reuters.com/article/us-refugees-media/bigotry-panic-reflected-in-media-coverage-of-migrants-and-refugees-idUSKBN0U129620151218. Accessed 31 October 2017.

Reuters. (2018). *Journalist Faked His Own Death Using Pig's Blood and Make-Up Artist.* https://www.smh.com.au/world/europe/journalist-faked-his-own-death-using-pig-s-blood-and-make-up-artist-20180601-p4ziry.html. Accessed 1 June 2018.

Robinson, P. (2011, April). The CNN Effect Reconsidered: Mapping a ResearchAgenda for the Future. *Media, War & Conflict, 4*(1), 3–11.

Rogers, James. (2012). *Reporting Conflict.* Hampshire: Palgrave Macmillan.

Said, E. (1978). *Orientalism.* London: Routledge & Kegan Paul.

Sambrook, R. (2010). Are Foreign Correspondents Redundant?: The Changing Face of International News. *Challenges.* Reuters Institute for the Study of Journalism. Oxford: Oxford University Press. https://reutersinstitute.politics.ox.ac.uk/sites/default/files/2017-12/Are%20Foreign%20Correspondents%20Redundant%20The%20changing%20face%20of%20international%20news.pdf. Accessed 30 December 2017.

Sammartino, Steve. (2017). *The Lessons School Forgot.* Milton, QLD: Wiley.

SBS. (2016, November 24). *How Meditation Is Helping the Middle East Achieve Zen.* http://www.sbs.com.au/topics/life/culture/article/2016/11/21/how-meditation-helping-middle-east-achieve-zen. Accessed 22 October 2017.

SBS. (2016, November 25). *How Zumba Is Helping Syrian Refugee Women to Heal.* http://www.sbs.com.au/topics/life/culture/article/2016/11/16/how-zumba-helping-syrian-refugee-women-he. Accessed 22 October 2017.

SBS Charter. https://www.sbs.com.au/aboutus/corporate/index/id/25/h/SBS-Charter. Accessed 1 May 2018.

Stecula, D. (2017, July 27). The Real Consequences of Fake News. *The Conversation.* https://theconversation.com/the-real-consequences-of-fake-news-81179. Accessed 28 May 2018.

Stratton, Jon. (2007). *Australian Rock: Essays on Popular Music.* Perth: Network Books.

The India Express. (2017, October 27). Transgender Policy Cleared by Karnataka Cabinet. http://indianexpress.com/article/india/transgender-policy-cleared-by-karnataka-cabinet-4909196/. Accessed 27 May 2018.

Thussu, D. K. (2004). Media Plenty and the Poverty of News. In C. Paterson & A. Sreberny (Eds.), *International News in the Twenty-First Century* (pp. 47–61). Eastleigh: John Libby Publishing.

Trenore, M. J. (2014, September 2). How Constructive Journalism Can Improve the Way Media Makers Tell Stories. *IVOH*. http://ivoh.org/constructive-journalism/. Accessed 14 April 2018.

UNESCO Report by the International Commission for the Study of Communication Problems. (1980). *Communication and Society Today and Tomorrow, Many Voices One World: Towards a New More Just and More Efficient World Information and Communication Order*. London: Kogan Page; New York: Unipub; Paris: UNESCO.

UNESCO World Report. (2009). *Investing in Cultural Diversity and Intercultural Dialogue*. http://www.un.org/en/events/culturaldiversityday/pdf/Investing_in_cultural_diversity.pdf. Accessed 29 October 2017.

Ward, S. (2010). *Global Journalism Ethics*. Montreal: McGill-Queen's University Press.

Weaver, D. H. (2005). Who Are Journalists? In H. de Burgh (Ed.), *Making Journalists: Diverse Models, Global Issues* (pp. 44–57). Florence: Taylor & Francis.

Williams, K. (2011). *International Journalism*. London: Sage.

Williams, M. (2018, June 2). Ukraine's Credibility Under Scrutiny Over Faked Murder. *Sydney Morning Herald*. https://www.smh.com.au/world/europe/ukraine-s-credibility-under-scrutiny-over-faked-murder-20180602-p4zj3j.html. Accessed 26 May 2018.

Worlds of Journalism. (2012–2016). *Aggregated Tables for Key Variables*. http://www.worldsofjournalism.org/research/2012-2016-study/data-and-key-tables/. Accessed 19 May 2018.

Zelizer, B. (2005). The Culture of Journalism. In C. James & G. Michael (Eds.), *Mass Media and Society* (4th ed., pp. 198–214). New York: Hodder Arnold.

INDEX

A
Advertising, 10
Africa, 33, 36, 57, 66
Al Jazeera, 30, 35, 39, 57
Amanpour, Christiane, 50
American, 53
Arab, 38, 39, 71, 73, 91, 93
Arab Spring, 24
Artificial intelligence, 18, 19
Asia, 24, 57, 66
Associated Press (AP), 43
Audiences, 2, 5, 10–12, 16, 21, 26,
    29–31, 33, 42, 46, 49–61, 66,
    68, 70, 71, 76–81, 88, 92, 95,
    96, 98, 105
Australian, 16, 35, 38, 40–42, 54, 73,
    81, 85, 86, 96, 97
Australian Broadcasting Service
    (ABC), 54
Authoritative, 31, 43

B
Bad news, 16, 77
BBC, 30, 58, 87

Bearing witness. *See* Witness
Beirut, 36
Blogs, 10, 15, 17
    bloggers. *See* Blogs
Borders, 25, 67, 70, 75, 93, 104
Bosnian war, 50
Breaking news, 27, 34, 45, 60

C
CCTV-9, 57
Channel News Asia, 57
Citizen journalist, 3, 5, 24, 44
CNN, 3, 5, 30, 50
Commercial, 16
Communities of interest, 54
Compassion fatigue, 77, 78
Conflict, 3, 4, 6, 18, 28, 30, 38, 44, 50,
    61, 67, 77, 79, 81, 93, 98, 104
Constructive journalism, 78–80
Cosmopolitan, 27
    cosmopolitanism. *See* Cosmopolitan
Crowdsourcing, 24
Culture of journalism, 66, 67, 69–71,
    73, 74

© The Editor(s) (if applicable) and The Author(s) 2019
S. Bebawi and M. Evans, *The Future Foreign Correspondent*,
https://doi.org/10.1007/978-3-030-01668-5

118   INDEX

D
Data journalism, 13
Dead Sea, 91–94
Diaspora, 46
Digital disruption, 9
Digital sphere, 27, 45
Discourse, 4–6, 25, 27, 29, 32–35, 37,
    38, 43, 51–54, 56–58, 61, 65–67,
    69, 71–73, 75, 81, 88, 90, 91,
    93, 94, 97, 104
    discourses. *See* Discourse
Dissemination, 15, 26, 27, 45
Diversity, 5, 12, 25, 27, 38, 69, 86,
    105
Domestic, 25, 26, 29, 98
Dominant media, 52

E
Economic, 21, 24, 25, 31, 37, 40, 45,
    57, 65, 76, 104
Editor, 3, 23, 24, 32, 33, 52, 55, 76,
    77
    editorial. *See* Editor
Embedded, 3, 5, 19, 28, 52, 93
Ethnicity, 46

F
Facebook, 11, 15–17, 75, 103
Facetime, 24
Fact-checking, 18, 19
Fake news, 1, 4, 5, 17, 50, 56, 60, 61,
    67, 102
Fisk, Robert, 36
Fixers, 39, 72, 88
Flows, 4, 12–14, 24, 27, 29,
    103–107

G
Gaddafi, Muammar, 44
Gender, 46, 97

Global, 14, 15, 17, 24, 25, 29, 30,
    32, 35, 42, 46, 47, 51, 53, 54,
    56–60, 69–73, 77, 78, 81, 86, 98
    globalisation. *See* Global
Global North, 4
Global South, 4, 24, 40, 57, 76, 81
Global sphere, 51
Globonews, 56
Government, 31, 35, 37, 44, 58, 72,
    77, 86
Gulf Times, 23
Gulf War, 31

H
Happy news, 4, 6, 16, 67, 76, 81, 82
Hierarchy of Influences model, 69, 70

I
Ideology, 3, 26
Indian, 36, 40–42, 57, 96, 97
Instagram, 15
Intercultural, 3, 4, 17, 29, 35, 47, 67,
    69, 86, 87, 91, 92, 97, 98, 105,
    106
International, 4, 15, 16, 25–32,
    35, 43–47, 49, 51, 53, 54, 56,
    58–60, 67–71, 76, 77, 82, 86,
    91, 97, 98, 105
    international journalism. *See*
    International
Investigative journalism, 57–59

J
Jordan, viii, 33, 38, 58, 73–75, 81, 82,
    86–88, 90, 91, 93, 97, 104

L
Latin America, 66
Legacy media, 9, 11

Libya, 44
Libyan. *See* Libya
Local, vii, viii, 4, 14, 25, 26, 28, 30,
    35–37, 39–43, 46, 47, 51–55,
    57–60, 68, 69, 71, 73–76, 81,
    82, 88, 89, 91, 92, 95, 97, 98,
    102, 105

M
MacBride report, 56
Media power, 29, 52, 70
Media rituals, 52
Mediate, 29, 30, 33, 34, 51, 75, 86
    mediating. *See* Mediate
Meditation, 87, 91–95
Middle East, 33, 36, 53, 57, 58, 74,
    81, 82, 87, 90, 93, 95
Multicultural, 46, 86

N
National, 16, 25–27, 46, 51–54, 95
News, 2, 4, 6, 10–12, 14–18, 25–27,
    30, 32, 33, 35–40, 43–46, 49,
    51–58, 60, 61, 65–73, 75–82,
    85, 87, 90, 91, 93, 97, 102, 105
News agenda, 43, 56, 60, 71, 75, 77
Newspapers, 11, 23, 35, 54, 55

O
Objective, 1, 16, 26, 39, 50, 79, 86,
    102
'Other', The, 53, 54, 78, 82, 86, 105

P
Parachute journalism, 36, 37, 60
Philippines, 37, 59, 86
Phoenix News, 57
Positive news, 69, 79
Producer, viii, 16, 39, 67, 95

R
Reality, 4, 5, 29, 31, 33, 35, 38, 39,
    46, 49–58, 60, 61, 65, 67, 72,
    73, 81, 90
Refugees, 53, 87–89, 92
Reuters, 2, 37, 39, 40, 59, 90
Robots, 2, 14, 107
Russia, 2

S
Said, Edward, 53, 78
Share Wars, 15
Skype, 24
Social media, 11, 15, 24, 25, 44
Social reality, 30, 52, 56, 71, 92
Solutions journalism, 78–80
Sourcing, 45
South Africa Broadcasting Cooperation
    (*SABC*), 57
Special Broadcasting Service (SBS), vii,
    32, 86, 87
Sphere, 4–6, 15, 32–34, 60, 67, 72,
    75, 78, 97, 98
Syria, 90, 93
    Syrian. *See* Syria

T
Technology, 11, 12, 18–21, 26, 45,
    46, 71
Telesur, 57
Todo Noticias, 57
Transcultural spheres, 5, 6, 28, 30, 34,
    37, 57, 61, 65–67, 69–71, 73–76,
    78, 86, 98, 101
Transgender, 87, 95–97,
    105
Transnational, 5, 6, 25, 27, 67, 78,
    98
Truth, 2, 3, 11, 16, 17, 50, 77, 79,
    105
Twitter, 15, 24

U
U.S. *See* American
Ukraine, 2
UNESCO, 56, 67–69
User-generated content, 15, 16

V
Virtual reality (VR), 17
Vox pops, 24

W
War. *See* Conflict
Western, 2, 12, 24, 39, 56, 57, 66, 68,
    69, 71, 74, 76, 77, 81, 82, 86,
    88, 90, 92, 94, 95, 97, 104

Witness, 30, 31
World Economic Forum, 11
Worlds of Journalism Study, 69

Y
YouTube, 15

Z
Zoom, 24
Zumba, 54, 87–92

Printed by Printforce, the Netherlands